An interpretation of Beethoven's *Symphony No. 5* by BERNARD LAMOTTE.
From the Capehart Collection.

World MUSIC HORIZONS

OSBOURNE McCONATHY · RUSSELL V. MORGAN
JAMES L. MURSELL · MARSHALL BARTHOLOMEW
MABEL E. BRAY · EDWARD BAILEY BIRGE
W. OTTO MIESSNER

SPECIAL MATERIAL BY
Marion Bauer AND *Charles Leonhard*

Silver Burdett Company

NEW YORK   CHICAGO   DALLAS   SAN FRANCISCO

ACKNOWLEDGMENTS

Without the help and cooperation of many persons and organizations, the publication of this book would not have been possible. Space limitations permit no more than the listing of some who have contributed to this enterprise. To these and to the many who go unnamed, the editors offer their sincere appreciation:

Nathan Krevitsky, Instructor of Art Education, Teachers College, Columbia University, for research in connection with the art work.

Marion Bauer, eminent composer, author, and lecturer, for the Listening Notes.

Edna W. Doll, Department of Physical Education, Clifford J. Scott High School, East Orange, New Jersey, for the Dance Program.

Charles Leonhard, Assistant Professor of Music Education, Teachers College, Columbia University, for the Music Reading Program.

Solomon Braslavsky, Musical Director, Temple Mishkan Tefila, Boston; Rev. Martin J. Burne, O.S.B., St. Mary's Abbey, Newark, N. J.; Frank Dunsmore, Edgemont School, Scarsdale, N. Y.; Rabbi Jacob Freedman, member of the National Jewish Music Committee as a Representative of the Synagogue Council of America; Luther Goodhart, New York University; Alfred H. Johnson, Park View School, Washington, D. C.; Frank Rehman, Director of Music, Garden City (N. Y.) Public Schools; and Ira Singleton, New York University, for research and consultation.

The Capehart-Farnsworth Corporation, who commissioned outstanding painters to translate onto canvas interpretations of some of the universally great music, is duly afforded grateful appreciation for permission to reproduce some of the paintings in the Capehart Collection.

Special acknowledgment and credit are due for permission to reprint the following:

"All Through the Night": Copyright, 1903, by G. Schirmer, Inc. Copyright renewed, 1931. Renewal copyright assigned to G. Schirmer, Inc. Printed by permission.

"Ba-A M'Nucha": Words from *Gems of Hebrew Verse*, translated from the original tongue by Harry H. Fein. Copyright 1940 by Bruce Humphries, Inc. Used by permission.

"Hatikvah": Modern English version by Rabbi Jacob Freedman.

"I Ride an Old Paint": Words and melody from *The American Songbag*, by Carl Sandburg. Used by permission of Harcourt, Brace and Company, Inc.

"I Vow to Thee, My Country": By permission, from Curwen Edition No. 71632, published by J. Curwen & Sons, Ltd., 24 Berners Street, London, W. 1.

"Mournful Serenade" ("Bella Fata"): Melody reprinted from *Eco di Napoli*, Vol. III, by permission of the publishers, G. Ricordi & Co.

"O God, Beneath Thy Guiding Hand": Descant from *34 Hymn Tune Descants* by David McK. Williams. Used by permission of The H. W. Gray Co.

"Peter": Copyright, 1939, by G. Schirmer, Inc. Used by permission.

"Saleynu": English translation used by permission of Harry H. Fein.

"Schnitzelbank": Melody and words from *German Folk Songs With Words*, used by permission of O. Pagani & Bro., Inc.

"This Is the Day": Words reprinted from *Eighteen Poems* by James Boyd; copyright 1944, by Charles Scribner's Sons. Used by permission of the publishers.

"Three Little Maids": Reprinted in this book by special permission of Chappell & Co., Limited, 1263 Bay Street, Toronto, Canada, copyright owners. All rights reserved.

"Thrush Song": Words from *A Boy's Book of Rhyme* by Clinton Scollard.

"Ute Mountain Air": Melody from *Northern Ute Music* (Bureau Bulletin 75) by Frances Densmore, published by the Bureau of American Ethnology.

"Vidalita": From *Canciones Típicas* by Irma Labastille, copyright, 1941, Silver Burdett Co.

"Watch America": Words reprinted from *The Darkening Meadow* by Robert Nathan, by permission of Alfred A. Knopf, Inc.

TABLE OF CONTENTS

ILLUSTRATIONS

Interpretation of Beethoven's *Symphony No. 5* by Bernard Lamotte, *frontispiece*

Interpretation of Liszt's *Hungarian Rhapsody No. 1 in F* by Robert Riggs, *30*

Manchester Valley by Joseph Pickett, *96*

Die Fledermaus, photographed in color during a production in Central City, Colorado, *130*

Journey of the Magi by Sassetta, *164*

Interpretation of Mozart composing *The Magic Flute* by Julian Levi, *198*

Interpretation of Falla's *The Three-Cornered Hat* by Julio de Diego, *232*

The United States Marine Band on the steps of the Capitol, Washington, D. C., *249*

Arturo Toscanini and the NBC Symphony Orchestra, *250*

INTRODUCTION

In planning and developing this book the authors have kept your interests, as a junior high school student, constantly in mind. They realize that you have many interests in common with your classmates and with young people in all parts of the world and that in many ways you are alike. They also recognize that each of you is an individual with your own distinctive tastes and your own particular abilities and goals.

The authors believe that you will find in this book materials and an organization that are adaptable to your interests as an individual, to your needs as a member of a group, and to the special concerns of your teachers. They hope that this book will increase your enjoyment and understanding of music, and that it will help you to grow, through music, into a broader, more self-sufficient, and understanding person.

While the music and related materials are grouped into sections called "A World View of Music," "Music in These United States," "Operetta on the International Stage," and so on, it is not necessary to follow this organization. You will probably want to dip into this section for one song, into another for a particular dance or for some specific information about musical instruments, and still another for one of Miss Bauer's interesting discussions about various instrumental compositions.

Your class may be interested in music that is related to other phases of your school work. If so, you will find that the wide variety of music included in the book makes it particularly valuable for such use. Again, you may be anxious to develop skill in music reading. In that case, you will find a practical music reading program offered for this specific purpose in the resource section of the book (page 251).

Whatever your musical interests may be — singing, instrumental music, dancing, composing, or technical aspects of music—you will find material to satisfy your needs. The authors hope that your musical interests and activities will be many-sided and well-rounded and will grow in both breadth and depth.

The songs in this book were selected and arranged with a view to providing you with varied musical experiences. There are fun songs, songs in the vein of current popular tunes, folk songs, classics, songs by contemporary composers. You will find some that appeal to you now, and others that you will grow to like as you get better acquainted with them. You will find solo songs, duets, three-part songs, four-part songs, rounds, and songs with descants (added melodies). But remember this: most of the songs can be easily adapted to varied situations. If, for example, your group is not large enough or advanced enough to sing a four-part song, there is no reason why you should not sing it anyway. The chances are that it is also a good three-part, or two-part, or even unison song. The Index (page 261) will show you the various voice combinations that are possible with the different songs in the book. If you choose the song, *One Quiet Night*, page 86, the Arrangement Index tells you it may be sung in unison, in two parts (S.A. or S.A./T.), in three parts (S.A.B.), or in four parts (S.A.T.B. or S.A.A./T.B.).

Some of the music that you learn in this book will be with you for the rest of your life. Some of it will stimulate you to further musical explorations and discoveries. Whatever your major concerns in life may be, music can be one of your most satisfying and constant sources of pleasure and comfort.

All-Time Songs

Sing out, my Soul, thy songs of joy;
    Such as a happy bird will sing
Beneath a Rainbow's lovely arch
    In early spring.

Sing, happy Soul, thy songs of joy;
    Such as a Brook sings in the wood,
That all night has been strengthened by
    Heaven's purer flood.

Songs of Joy
W. H. DAVIES

Man sings not only joyful songs but also songs of love, of sorrow, of country, of God. Usually his songs come into being, live for a while, and are forgotten. But occasionally a song comes along which people like so well that they keep it alive, and in this way it is shared with people of other lands and later times. Songs like this endure because, as the English poet, William Wordsworth, said over a hundred years ago, they are "Old songs, the precious music of the heart." Such songs do more than entertain and please temporarily; they have a quality that goes straight to the heart. To us, they are like old friends; the longer we know them, the closer we feel to them. And the closer we feel to them, the more we understand and enjoy them. They are our songs and our friends' songs. We know them so well that we sing them by heart.

The songs in this section have been called "All-Time Songs" because they have lived in the hearts and minds and voices of many people for a long time. And they will continue, no doubt, to live for a much longer time.

No one knows where the oldest songs came from. Maybe some untrained singer thought them up while he followed the plow, as Robert Burns thought up some of his poetry. Or the songs we know may have been the results of many people's singing over, and changing gradually, a simple melody that someone started. Nowadays, popular song writers sometimes borrow tunes from the great symphonies and concertos. On the other hand, the composers of symphonies and concertos frequently use folk songs for some of the melodies in their large works.

The great composer, Beethoven, whose *Fifth Symphony* inspired the painting by *Bernard Lamotte* at the front of this book, used the first song in the book, *Lord Thy Glory,* in his final symphony, the ninth. And the greatest composer of church music, Johann Sebastian Bach, harmonized and used *All Glory, Laud and Honor* more than two hundred years ago.

Country Gardens is based on a very old and popular English dance song. It has been arranged and made even more famous by the composer and pianist, Percy Grainger.

Morning is an Italian song that has been sung in Italy and other European countries for many years.

Annie Laurie and the American Negro spiritual, *Deep River,* are too familiar a part of our heritage here in the United States to need any comment.

You may not know all these songs; you probably do not. But make them your songs. As you sing them over and over again, you will feel their strength and beauty. Sing them as they are written or sing them in unison. They are satisfying and thrilling either way. When you sing them, think about the meaning of the words, and try to express this and the feeling of the music in your faces, in your bodies, and in your voices.

As you sing these songs, let your eyes and your posture show the sincerity of your feeling for the music you are singing. Feel relaxed, but strong and flexible, as if you could move easily and quickly in any direction without having to "change gears." Breathe deeply, but not forcefully, and sing with firm and free tones.

Listen closely to the music, and make your voice a part of it. If others are singing with you, let your voice blend with theirs to sound almost as one. And above all, enjoy the thrill of common purpose in singing together with your friends; in singing these beautiful songs that will soon become some of your favorite "All-Time Songs."

Lord, Thy Glory

From *Symphony No. 9* by Ludwig van Beethoven
Arranged by Herbert Haufrecht

Richard Mant

Allegro assai (♩ =126)

Lord, Thy glo - ry fills the heav - en; Earth is with its full - ness stored;

Un - to Thee be glo - ry giv - en, Ho - ly, ho - ly, ho - ly Lord!

Heav'n is still with an - thems ring - ing; Earth takes up the an - gels' cry,

"Ho - ly, ho - ly, ho - ly " sing - ing; "Lord of Hosts, Thou Lord most high."

Breth - ren raise your voic - es in praise! Oh, praise the Lord on

Ev - er thus in God's high prais - es, Breth - ren let our tongues u - nite,

high. Let's raise our voices in praise, Oh praise the Lord! Ah,

While our thought to His greatness rais-es, All our love His gifts ex-cite.

Ah,

With His ser-aph train be-fore Him; With His ho-ly church be-low,

Breth - ren raise your voic-es in praise, Oh let our an-them flow.

Thus u-nit-ed, we a-dore Him, Bid we thus our an-them flow.

Deep River

Negro Spiritual
Arranged by MARSHALL BARTHOLOMEW

Deep____ riv - er, my home is o - ver Jor - dan.

Hum____

Con ped.

Deep____ riv - er, Lord, I want to cross o - ver in - to camp-ground.

I want to cross o - ver in - to camp-ground.

poco piu mosso

Oh, don't you want__ to go__ to that gos - pel__ feast,__ To that

Oh, don't you want to go to that gos - pel _ feast,__ To that

poco piu mosso

ped.

5

Morning

Eleanor Graham Vance

F. Paolo Tosti

1. Morn - ing! It's morn - ing! Earth gives its greet - ing, Moun - tain and
2. Morn - ing! It's morn - ing! Birds trill their glad - ness, Pour - ing their
3. Morn - ing! It's morn - ing! Join in the sing - ing, Raise ev - 'ry

mead - ow e - merge from shades of night. Ban - ished by sun - rise, the
hearts out in car - ols sweet and gay. Gone with the night - time are
voice in a tune - ful song of cheer. Sing till the ech - oes are

dark - ness is fleet - ing. Earth's ev - 'ry crea - ture Wel - comes the dawn - ing,
sor - row and sad - ness. Bright as the dawn - ing, Faith is re - newed each
hap - pi - ly ring - ing. Sing to the morn - ing! Sing for the day is

light. Earth's ev - 'ry crea - ture Wel - comes the dawn - ing light.
day. Bright as the dawn - ing, Faith is re - newed each day.
here! Sing to the morn - ing! Sing for the day is here!

7

Annie Laurie

WILLIAM DOUGLASS

LADY JOHN SCOTT
Arr. by OSBOURNE WILLIAM MCCONATHY

9

Country Gardens

English Folk Song
Arranged by HERBERT HAUFRECHT

HERBERT HAUFRECHT

Moderato (♩ =138)

mf

crescendo

f

allargando

mf

mf

Win - ter is gone, and now we have spring; To the fields we go to work and sing.

mf a tempo

f

Heigh-ho! We go, We'll plough and we'll sow; To the fields we're off with spade and hoe.

f

f

as   we plant,_With the day   fair and bright, we'll work un-til   the night, When the

plant - ing's done we'll dance and chant.   Win - ter is gone,   and

now   we have spring,_____ We're off   to   work   and   sing.

To the fields we're off   to   work   and sing. It's with a

Fa la la la la la la la _____ We're off with
heigh - ho! we go, We'll plough and we'll sow, To the fields we're off with

To the fields, _____
spade and hoe. We go with spade and hoe, to the

We sing heigh - ho, heigh - ho!
fields we sing heigh - ho! Heigh - ho!
We sing heigh - ho, heigh - ho!

13

All Glory, Laud, and Honor

JOHN MASON NEALE

TESCHNER—BACH
Arranged by HERBERT HAUFRECHT

sempre dim.

in — the Lord's name com - est, Thou King and Bless - ed One.

sempre dim.

f Descant (optional)

To Thee be - fore Thy pas - sion They sang their hymns of praise; To

To Thee be - fore Thy pas - sion They sang their hymns of praise; To

Thee now high ex - alt - ed Our mel - o - dy we raise. Thou

Thee now high ex - alt - ed Our mel - o - dy we raise. Thou —

15

didst ac - cept their prais - es, Ac - cept the praise we bring, Who

didst ac - cept their prais - es, Ac - cept the praise we bring, Who

in all good de - light - est, Thou good and gra - cious King, Thou

in all good de - light - est, Thou good and gra - cious King, Thou

good and gra - cious King! A - men.

good and gra - cious King! A - men.

Form in Music

When you listen to a piece of music, or sing it, or play it, or dance to it, you are likely to be aware that it is constructed according to a plan. This plan or scheme is what we call the "form" of the music. *The Star-Spangled Banner* is a good example of musical form. Notice how it is put together.

First there are the four opening lines:

"O say! can you see, by the dawn's early light,
What so proudly we hailed at the twilight's
　last gleaming?
Whose broad stripes and bright stars, through
　the perilous fight,
O'er the ramparts we watched, were so gal-
　lantly streaming!"

The music to which these lines are sung seems to make up a single and rather compact section. Then, when the next two lines come in, it changes to something quite different:

"And the rockets' red glare, the bombs bursting
　in air,
Gave proof through the night that our flag was
　still there."

Then with the closing lines, there is still another change in the music.

"O say, does that Star-Spangled Banner yet
　wave
O'er the land of the free and the home of the
　brave?"

The whole song is made up of three sections, each one a little different from the rest, yet all belonging together.

Everyone who listens, sings, plays, or dances is more or less conscious of form in music. It is something that a person can hardly miss completely. If you notice the form of a piece of music when you are listening to it, you will find that the music becomes far more enjoyable and interesting to you. But this will not be the only result. If you notice the form of a piece that you are singing or playing, it will help you to find ways of making the music sound better.

You can see at once that this is so if you remember how a fine military band plays *The Star-Spangled Banner*. Nearly all the instruments of the band play the music of the first four lines. Then, for the next two lines, many of the instruments stop playing and the music becomes much softer, but it swells out again on the words:

"our flag was still there."

With the closing lines all of the instruments play, including the tympani which have not been used up to that point. You know very well what a thrilling effect this makes. Our national anthem sounds much better and more impressive when played in this way than it does when heard evenly and without any changes at all. And the whole secret lies in noticing the plan or form of the music, and in playing it so as to make that form or plan more clear.

Another good example is *Old Folks at Home*. Its plan or form is different from that of *The Star-Spangled Banner*, although it also has three parts. The first of these parts goes like this:

" 'Way down upon the Swanee River,
　Far, far away,
There's where my heart is turning ever,
　There's where the old folks stay."

Then the same music is repeated with different words:

"All up and down the whole creation,
　Sadly I roam,
Still longing for the old plantation,
　And for the old folks at home."

All of the music thus far makes up the first part or section of the song. Then something decidedly different makes up the second part:

"All the world is sad and dreary,
　Ev'rywhere I roam."

Then finally we have:

"Oh, brothers, how my heart grows weary,
　Far from the old folks at home!"

Notice that this last section of the song is a repetition. It brings in once again the last of the music of the first part. This kind of plan or form where a tune or musical idea is repeated once, twice, and even several times is very common in music. You will not find such repetitions in *The Star-Spangled Banner* because it is built on a different plan and has a different form. Yet in *Old Folks at Home* also, the form can be used to make the music more enjoyable and effective. You might, perhaps, sing the whole of the first section quite softly, getting even softer as the section comes to an end on the line:

"There's where the old folks stay."

Then in the middle section you might let the sound swell out, making it die away to the merest whisper in the closing section. This would be one way, although certainly not the only way, of bringing out the form; and you can see at once how it would help to "put the song across" with an audience, and to make the singing of it more enjoyable.

The particular form of which *Old Folks at Home* is an example is often called the *A-B-A* form because there is a first section, a somewhat contrasting middle section, and a closing section which repeats at least some of the first. *Old Folks at Home* was written by Stephen Foster. Sing through two other songs by him which you will find in this book. They are *Oh! Susanna* (page 26) and *Massa's in the Cold, Cold Ground* (page 22). You will find that their general plan is the same — *A-B-A*.

If you think through other songs you know well and examine the music of still others in this book, you will find that many of them are in this *A-B-A* form. When you listen to instrumental music, you will find that a great deal of it, too, is in this form.

Now let us turn to something different. Hum through *America* and see if you can tell how it is constructed. You will notice that it has two parts. The first part goes with the lines:

"My country, 'tis of thee,
Sweet land of liberty,
Of thee I sing;"

The second part goes with the lines:

"Land where my fathers died!
Land of the Pilgrims' pride!
From every mountain side,
Let freedom ring!"

Instead of repetition here, you see two more or less contrasting musical ideas, one after the other. So this is often called the *A-B* or two-part form. This is the form of the song *When Love Is Kind* (page 21).

"When Love is kind, cheerful and free,
Love's sure to find welcome from me."

There is part one! Right away there follows part two:

"But when Love brings heartache and pang,
Tears and such things, Love can go hang."

This is a particularly good example, because the moment you notice the form of *When Love Is Kind* you get the idea of singing the two sections quite differently, which is just what you ought to do.

All composers build their music according to plan. The reason why they do this is not necessarily because the rules say they should. They do it in order to make their music more interesting and enjoyable. The great Wolfgang Amadeus Mozart once wrote a very interesting letter to his father about this very point. In this letter he told his father all about the first performance of one of his symphonies. He explained that near the start of the symphony he had brought in a passage which he was sure was going to please the audience. He brought it in very quietly because he thought that this would attract special attention. But he was so certain that it would make a hit that he decided to introduce it once more, right at the end. This second time it was to be played as loudly as possible. Sure enough, everyone sat up and took notice when the theme came in the first time; some people even clapped. But when the passage burst forth once more at the end, blared out by the full orchestra, the effect was terrific, and there was a storm of applause.

So you see, when you pay attention to the form of a piece of music, you are noticing something that the composer hoped you would notice. It is something that can give you pleasure as well as help you to make the music sound better if you are singing or playing it.

There is nothing strange about getting pleasure from the form of a piece of music, for form does a great deal to increase enjoyment in all the other arts as well.

Take poetry, for example. No doubt you have read Edgar Allan Poe's famous poem, *The Raven*. You remember how the word "nevermore" comes in again and again in the last line of many of the verses, but not always in exactly the same way. Sometimes it is the raven himself who says "nevermore," but not always. These repetitions, with a certain amount of change, do a great deal for the effect of the poem.

Poe, the author of the poem, has actually told us that he worked out this pattern for a very definite purpose. He wanted his poem to produce an effect of melancholy or sadness. He thought that the word "nevermore" would be ideal for producing such an effect because it has a melancholy sound and a sad meaning. So he deliberately built his poem around this word. That is, he planned a definite form for his poem because he wanted it to make a definite impression on those who would read it. You may find it interesting to notice how much form or general arrangement has to do with the effect of other poems.

Then, too, much of the impression made upon us by buildings and pictures depends upon their form or arrangement. The Capitol in Washington, D. C., has two wings connected by a central section, with the great dome in the middle, and the stairway sweeping upwards. It was not planned in this way just for the sake of housing Congress conveniently. Indeed, it is probably not a very convenient building. But the orderliness, regularity, and formality of its plan seem to speak of the dignity of our country and the majesty of its government.

In many fine churches all the windows and doorways and arches come to a peak, and there is a spire soaring above everything toward a peak. All these details together are part of the form of the building, and they tend to carry both our eyes and our thoughts upward, which, of course, is precisely their purpose.

The picture on page 164 of this book, "Journey of the Magi" by Sassetta, makes an interesting pattern. The main movement is a strong diagonal from right to left; but notice the pattern of motion within this major design. The man in the blue coat at the extreme left is facing back into the picture, as well as the man in the scarlet coat just above him. Between them a little dog carries along the main motion. The artist accomplishes two purposes with this delicate balance. First, the eye is pleased with the variety within the pattern, and interest is focused on the main figure — the three men (the Magi) who appear with golden halos. Then, notice how the main theme, the procession, is set against relatively quiet spaces, the purposely simplified hills. In this way, the artist emphasizes the liveliness of the main theme.

In the same manner, a composer places slow and lively music in sequence. Again, as the musician would repeat a theme for special accent, so Sassetta repeats his scarlets, clear blues, and gold in a carefully regulated pattern. Notice how the main theme carries the richer, brighter colors, while the background of grey, brown, and rose lends depth and quietness to the scene.

Just as you can find patterns within patterns in the Sassetta picture and in many other pictures as well, you can also find them in music. For instance, the opening section of *Oh! Susanna* is itself made up of two parts. The first of them goes with the words:

"I came from Alabama with my banjo on my
      knee,
I'm goin' to Louisiana my true love for to see;"
Then the same music comes in again to the words:
"It rained all night the day I left,
      The weather it was dry;
The sun so hot I froze to death,
      Susanna, don't you cry."

Indeed we can go even further, for each of these smaller parts is made up of two still smaller and shorter ones. Sing the first two lines:
"I came from Alabama
      With my banjo on my knee,"
You will notice that the music does not seem to reach a closing point on the word "knee." You have the feeling that it ought to go on. Sure enough, it does, with the words:
"I'm goin' to Louisiana
      My true love for to see;"
Here the tune of the first two lines is repeated again — almost! But there is a small, yet very important, difference. On the word "see" the music does seem to come to a natural ending.

Turn now to the second main section of the song:
"Oh! Susanna, oh don't you cry for me."
It is a very short section, but it stands out by itself, and you certainly seem to feel it that way. Yet short though it is, it, too, is made up of two parts: "Oh! Susanna," and "oh don't you cry for me." And between these two there is an interesting contrast, for in the first the music goes up, and in the second it goes down.

One could go on at great length pointing out patterns within patterns in any piece of music. Once you are on the look-out for them, they are not hard to find. If you examine a number of the songs in this book, you will discover plenty of musical patterns within patterns for yourself. This is a very good thing to do, for when a person notices these details of form he can bring them out in the singing of the song.

Think of ways in which *Oh! Susanna* might be sung to bring out all the little repetitions and changes we have found in it. Sometimes you might sing louder, sometimes softer; sometimes you might go faster, sometimes slower; sometimes you might make a little pause. You can see how all this would help to put the song across with an audience. It is an important part of what we call interpreting the song. This is just what all fine musicians — pianists, instrumentalists, orchestra conductors — do with music. They are conscious of the big subdivisions of the music, and also of the smaller patterns within patterns which go to make up its form. They play the music so as to bring out its form.

So far we have said nothing about the technical terms that are used in talking about musical form. Yet these words are very useful, and it is well to know the most important of them.

Oh! Susanna, as we have seen, is made up of three parts, with some of the first section repeated right at the end. It is arranged in the order *A-B-A*, and sometimes this particular form is simply called the *A-B-A* form. Sometimes, too, it is called the *three-part* form, or *ternary* form. *America*, on the other hand, is made up of only two parts, arranged in the order *A-B*. This is usually called the *two-part* form, or *binary* form. There are many other types of musical form besides these, but we will not bother about them now, for the two we have discussed are the most basic of all.

Then there are technical names for the smaller musical subdivisions. The smallest musical pattern is called a *figure* and is usually from two to five notes in length. The first three notes of *The Star-Spangled Banner*, "O—say," make up one figure, and the next three, "can you see," another. With *Oh! Susanna* we might think of "I came from" as the first figure of the song, and "Alabama" as the next.

Figures combine into the motive, the musical pattern that is next in size. For example, together the first two figures of *The Star-Spangled Banner* make up the motive, "O—say! can you see," and the same thing is true of *Oh! Susanna*, "I came from Alabama."

Motives in turn group themselves into *phrases*. "O—say! can you see, by the dawn's early light," is the first phrase of *The Star-Spangled Banner*. "What so proudly we hailed at the twilight's last gleaming?" is the next. Notice how the end of both of these phrases gives a feeling of rest, but, as you can see, the ending of the second phrase is more complete. These points of rest are called *cadences*, and they vary in their degree of completeness. Usually we think of cadences as being *complete* or *incomplete*. Frequently, phrases are four measures long, but this is not always true, for they vary in length from two to eight measures. Since all phrases end with cadences, we can tell where they end by these points of rest.

You will find that phrases very often go together in pairs and that the second serves as a kind of answer to the first. Many theorists call these pairs of phrases *periods*. We might think of a period as a complete musical thought and of a phrase as a complete or incomplete thought, depending on whether its cadence is complete or incomplete. Periods combine with other periods or phrases into short pieces or into sections of larger works.

It will add to your enjoyment of music to learn to locate phrases and periods by eye, but when you do, you should also learn to hear what you see. In other words, you should know how the notes will sound when they are played or sung, so that you recognize form "by ear." It is only when you *hear* the phrases, the periods, and the variations of these patterns, that your understanding of music, and your pleasure in it, will be strengthened.

It is possible that you may enjoy diagramming some of the songs in this book. If you do, one way is to use capital letters for periods *A*, numbers for phrases *1*, small letters for motives *a*, and numbers in parentheses for figures *(1)*. This kind of work can be very enjoyable, for music can be as complicated and interesting as a jigsaw puzzle. But always remember that the real purpose of studying music in this technical way is to enable you to notice things about it that will make it possible for you to enjoy it more, and to perform and interpret it better.

When Love Is Kind

THOMAS MOORE

Irish Folk Song arranged by JOSEPH DEVAUX

Ah _____

Tears and such things, _____ Love may go hang!
To two or three, _____ then good-bye, Love!
For aught I care, _____ to Jer - i - cho!

Tears and such things, then __ Love may go hang!
To two or three, oh __ then good-bye, Love!
For aught I care, un- to Jer - i - cho!

Massa's in the Cold, Cold Ground

STEPHEN COLLINS FOSTER

STEPHEN COLLINS FOSTER
Arranged by JOSEPH DeVAUX

Andantino (♩ =84)

Oo _____ Oo _____ Oo _____

1. Round the mead-ows am a - ring - ing   The old one's mourn-ful   song,____
   Where the i - vy am a - creep - ing   ⁊   O'er the grass - y   mound,____
2. When the au-tumn leaves were fall - ing   ⁊   When the days were   cold,____ 'Twas
   Now the or-ange trees are bloom-ing   ⁊   On the sand - y   shore____

While the mock-ing-bird am sing - ing,   Hap-py as the day am   long.
Dare old mas-sa am a - sleep - ing,   Sleep-ing in the cold, cold ground.
Hard to hear old Mas-sa call - ing,   Cause he was so weak and old.
Now the sum-mer days are com - ing,   Mas-sa nev-er calls no more.

piu mosso   *rit.*

Down   in   de   corn - field   Hear dat mourn - ful   sound:

tempo primo

All   the old ones am a - weep - ing,   Mas-sa's in the cold, cold ground.

Old Folks at Home

STEPHEN COLLINS FOSTER

STEPHEN COLLINS FOSTER
Arranged by RUSSELL MORGAN

Andante (♩=92)

'Way down up-on the Swa-nee Riv-er,
All round the lit-tle farm I wan-dered

Far, far a-way,
When I was young,
There's where my heart is
Then man-y hap-py

turn-ing ev-er, There's where the old folks stay.
days I squan-dered, Man-y the songs I've sung.

All up and down the whole cre-a-tion, Sad-ly I
When I was play-ing with my broth-er, Hap-py was

Oh! Susanna

STEPHEN COLLINS FOSTER
Arranged by JOSEPH DeVaux

STEPHEN COLLINS FOSTER

sun so hot I froze to death; Su - san - na, don't you cry.

Oh, Su - san - na, Oh, don't you cry for me, I've

come from Al - a - ba - ma With my ban - jo on my knee.

INSTRUMENTS OF THE STRING FAMILY

Musical instruments belong to various groups that are sometimes called "families." The "string family" includes the familiar instruments that make up the string section of a symphony orchestra: violin, viola, cello, and double bass. The harp also belongs to this group, as do the guitar and mandolin and instruments similar to them. The piano is sometimes classed with this group.

Sometimes stringed instruments are divided into classes according to the way they are played: bowed, plucked, and struck.

When we talk of orchestral music, we think of the bowed instruments as the important members of the string family and the real backbone of the orchestra. The violin, at times, is called the soprano of the section because it usually plays the highest parts. Actually, the violins in an orchestra are divided into first and second violins because each group has its own separate part. It would be impossible to describe in words the great variety of expressive qualities of the violin, but there is general agreement that the instrument plays a very important part in both solo and orchestral music.

The violin's big sister, the viola, is five tones lower in pitch but lacks the flashiness of the star member of the family. Its tone quality is darker and more veiled and is not as brilliant as the violin. But the viola is well suited to the part it plays and is necessary as the alto of the string section.

The supporting star of the string section is the cello (violoncello). Some have likened its quality to the baritone voice, and others have called it the tenor or baritone of the orchestra. Because of its rich, mellow tone, composers have written some of their most appealing music for the cello.

The double bass, often referred to as string bass, is the lowest pitched member of the string family and also the largest. It is used in dance bands as well as in concert orchestras, and it always plays the lowest part.

In a good portion of early orchestral music, the double bass played the cello part an octave lower, but in most of the music we hear today each instrument has its own separate part. This means then that there are generally five individual parts in the string section. It also means that the instruments of the string section can supply the full melody and harmony of a composition, and often play without the other instruments.

Bowed instruments offer an interesting study in musical sound. As the bow is drawn across them, the strings vibrate the individual pitch sounds. These sounds, in turn, are made to sound much greater by the vibration of the air within the instrument.

The four modern stringed instruments are related closely to their immediate ancestors, the viols, which were in use during the 16th and 17th centuries. These instruments possessed soft, delicate tones, and they were far less powerful and brilliant than the modern stringed instruments.

Three important instruments of the "plucked" class that have long been known in music are the guitar, the mandolin, and the harp. The guitar is a descendant of Oriental instruments of many centuries ago. The mandolin is from the lute family so important to music three centuries ago. The harp, an ancient instrument, is used frequently for very beautiful effects in the modern orchestra. Of the instruments which are "struck," the best-known today is the piano, sometimes referred to as a percussion instrument. You may be interested in learning something about the forerunners of this most popular and useful instrument. They are the harpsichord and the clavichord.

The harpsichord is a harp-shaped instrument having a keyboard that produces its tones by the plucking of its strings with quill or leather points. Its soft tones blend well with the violin and other stringed instruments. The clavichord is closer to the modern piano because its strings were struck by small hammers, but its tone was also very small for a concert hall. The modern grand piano, although its essentials were invented by Christofori early in the 18th century, did not come into wide use until early in the 19th century.

A World View of Music

For doth not song
To the whole world belong?
Is it not given wherever tears can fall?
Wherever hearts can melt or blushes glow
Or mirth or sadness mingle as they flow,
A heritage to all?

ISA CRAIG KNOX

Song does belong to the world. Historians tell us that music has played an important part in the life of man as far back as we have any records of human existence. Some even think that music was used as a means of communication before language. But since we are interested in music that is alive today rather than in relics of the past, we will concern ourselves very little with history. The important thing is to find likenesses and differences in the music of various people *from their music*.

It is often said that one way to get to know a people is through their music. Let's explore this idea by briefly considering some of our own musical experiences.

When you wake up in the morning feeling cheerful and well, your morning "shower" song is likely to be bright and happy. It makes no difference whether you sing a song or just hum snatch phrases you make up, the mood is gay and spirited. You are content and satisfied, and your singing shows it. On the other hand, things occasionally may not be going so well. You feel irritable or unhappy. If you sing at all during times like this, your morning song is probably quite somber and melancholy. In your singing you have been expressing your feelings in sound, and these feelings are very probably due to your reaction to things about you.

The same thing is true of music of a people, or of a composer. The music of oppressed peoples is usually sad. Its effect on you is one of pathos and longing. To some extent the music of the far northern countries, where winters are cold and hard, is more somber and heavy than that of warmer countries.

Such everyday things as making a living, social customs, dances, and political events have their effect on music also. Here in the United States, for example, you will find considerable difference between the mood or feeling of the songs of cowboys and those of workers on southern plantations, and between the songs of lumberjacks in the north woods and those of coal miners in the southern mountains. Music reflects many things about the life of a people —their daily concerns, their hopes, fears, pride, resentments, leisure pursuits, and even their hatreds.

The songs in this section are representative of many peoples of the world. You will enjoy singing them because, first and foremost, they are good songs, well arranged. You will find that they are varied in mood, tempo, style, and subject matter. They are musical songs and should be sung in a musical manner. You will want to compare them so as to discover likenesses and differences. But you will also want to use them to gain greater understanding of the people in other parts of the world who composed and sang these songs.

You will enjoy listening to instrumental music by the leading composers of these other countries, for this is just as rewarding an experience as singing their songs. You may want to use your library to look up information about the people whose songs you sing and whose music you hear or play. And you certainly will enjoy learning as much as you can about their national dances.

The reproduction of the painting by Robert Riggs on the next page is an artist's interpretation of a gypsy dance.

The more you learn about other people in the world, the more you will appreciate your democratic heritage, and the more you will feel your responsibility as an American citizen. In the world today we feel that our only hope for peace lies in the spread of the democratic ideal. This means that all of us must have a better and more sympathetic understanding of our neighbors, both at home and across the seas. Music, you will find, can do much to help us gain such an understanding.

An interpretation of Liszt's *Hungarian Rhapsody No. 1 in F* by ROBERT RIGGS   From the Capehart Collection.

Pretty Jennee

Irish Folk Song
Arranged by Joseph DeVaux

1. In— Lein-ster there lived a young dam-sel,_____ Oh, a
2. Her— eyes they were shin-ing like dia-monds,_____ Their—
3. And— oh then her form is as grace-ful,_____ As—

beau-ti-ful crea-ture was she;_____ For— nev-er a
col-or was blue as the sea;_____ And— Cu-pid, all
Ve-nus who rose from the sea;_____ For— nev-er a

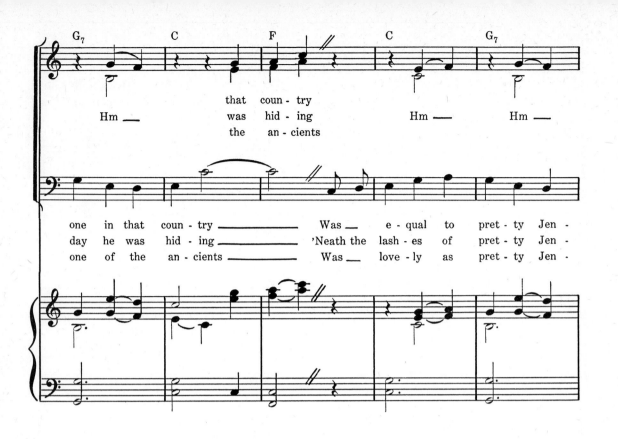

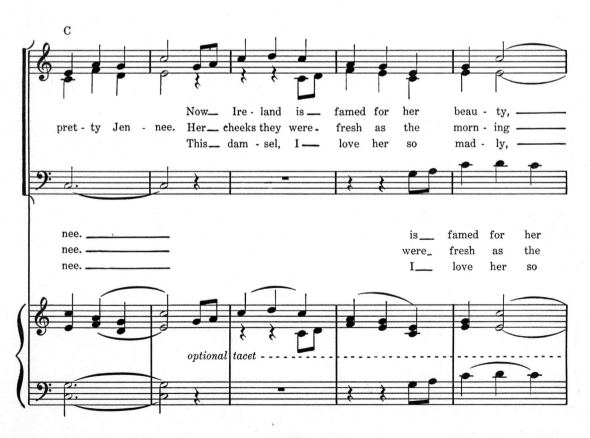

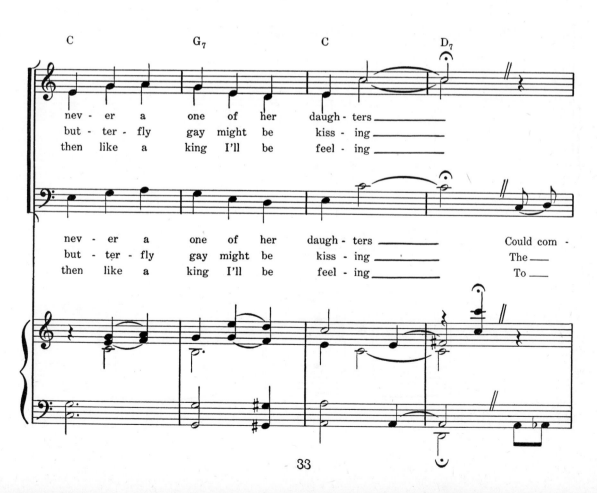

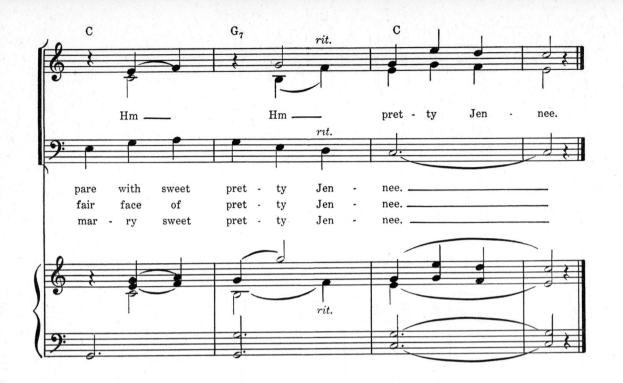

Hm —— Hm —— pret - ty Jen - nee.

pare with sweet pret - ty Jen - nee. ——————
fair face of pret - ty Jen - nee. ——————
mar - ry sweet pret - ty Jen - nee. ——————

The Spider's Web

CHARLOTTE DRUIT COLE °

PAUL HINDEMITH

Allegretto (♩ =108)

Spi - der! Spi - der! What are you spin - ning? A

cloak for a fair - y I'm just be - gin - ning.

What is it made of? Tell me true.
When will the fair - y be wear - ing it? To -

Threads of moon - shine and pearls of dew.
night, when the glow - worm lamps are

lit. Can I see her if I come peep - ing?

All good chil - dren must be then sleep - ing.

35

The Sierras of Chiapas

From the Spanish of José Munoz Cota
English version by Joseph DeVaux

Alfonso Esparza Oteo
Arranged by Joseph DeVaux

*In cases where piano accompaniments clash with the chording as given, either one or the other should be used, but not both.

Bid Phillis Goodbye

English version by
NANCY BYRD TURNER

French Folk Song
Arr. by OSBOURNE WILLIAM McCONATHY

Allegro moderato (♩ =112)

Why must you pine so for Phil - lis, a maid - en Fick - le as
Be not too faith - ful, ad - mir - ing her grac - es; Dark-eyed and

A - pril, now sun - light, now rain? Why, should you go with your heart heav - y -
change-ful, she laughs when you sigh. World's full of girls as a field's full of

lad - en Ask-ing her fa - vor and ask - ing in vain? — Why must you
dai - sies, Pick one of those and bid Phil - lis good - bye! — Be not too

Fine

Dal Segno

Long ago it was the fashion for poets to address the objects of their admiration by names taken from mythology or from the Latin poets. Their sonnets and madrigals celebrated the charms of Celia, Daphne, Amaryllis, Chloe, Cynthia, Iris, etc. Kings and queens, lords and ladies, and their attendants played at being shepherds and shepherdesses, dressed in fancy but impractical costumes. They used all kinds of poetical figures of speech.

All of this was charming, but wholly artificial and unreal. And the music that went with their songs was artificial; but still it was charming.

It did not reflect real emotion, but abounded in stilted measures and formal turns of expression. Not until Purcell did a composer dare to show in his music, the real emotions of human beings in relation to life. And it remained for Beethoven to free music from its traditional reticence and allow it to express the realities of human experience. Beethoven did this by writing music which expressed not only his struggle in the battle of life, but also the struggle of all mankind. *Lord, Thy Glory,* page 2, from Beethoven's *Ninth Symphony,* is a splendid example of his genius in musical composition.

Our Land

From the Finnish poem of
J. L. RUNEBERG

Finnish National Song by F. PACIUS
Arranged by MARSHALL BARTHOLOMEW

1. Our land, our land, our fa-ther-land, Thou glo-rious word ring forth! No
2. How blest, how pre-cious is this spot; The things we love are here. How-
3. But could we choose to dwell in light, In gold-en clouds of morn. Where

moun-tain ris-es proud and grand, Nor slopes a vale, nor sweeps a strand, More
ev-er hard may be our lot, A land, a fa-ther-land we've got. What
thou-sand stars are gleam-ing bright, Where tears are ab-sent, days are bright. Still

dear than thou land of the north, Our fa-ther's na-tive earth. No earth.
earth-ly bless-ings could com-pare? What place could be more dear? How dear?
for this land where life is stern Our long-ing souls would yearn! Where yearn!

The Dancing Maiden

English version by
ANN JOHNSON

Swedish Folk Song
Arranged by ANN JOHNSON

1. The maid danc-ing on the green held a red rib-bon band; The_ maid danc-ing on the green held a red rib-bon band;_ She tied it a - round her ad - mir - er's strong
2. "Now don't bind my arm so tight - ly, so tight - ly, my dear; Now_ don't bind my arm so tight - ly, so tight - ly, my dear;_ For I would-n't dream of es - cap - ing from
3. So, slow - ly she loosed the band, and her sweet-heart set free; So,_ slow - ly she loosed the band, and her sweet-heart set free;_ And off to the woods did her gen - tle - man

hand; She tied it a - round her ad - mir - er's strong hand.
here; For I would-n't dream of es - cap - ing from here."
flee! And off to the woods did her gen - tle - man flee!

The Queen's Prayer

From the Hawaiian of
QUEEN LILIUOKALANI

QUEEN LILIUOKALANI
Arranged by LAURA E. BROWN

Andante religioso (♩ =88)

p

1. Oh, Lord, Thy lov - ing grace __ has guard - ed all our ways; We have
2. Pro - tect our ev - 'ry thought;— for - give the wrong we've done; Grant us
1. O kou a - lo - ha no —— A - i - a - i ka - la - ni A
2. Mai na - na i - no i - no Na he - wa o ka - na - ka A

fol - lowed in Thy truth,__and for this, we of - fer praise. *pp*
peace and end - less mer - cy, and bless us, ev - 'ry one. A - men.—
o kou oi a - i - o He he - mo - le - le hoi. A - men - e.
ka e hu - i ka - la A ma - e ma - e no. A - men - e.

3. We humbly bow our heads
   And thank thee for thy care;
   Keep us mindful of thy glory
   Which all Thy works declare.

3. Na laila e ka Haku
   Malalo kou cheu
   Ko makou maluhia
   A mau loa aku no.

The Mournful Serenade

English version by
JOSEPH DEVAUX

Italian Folk Song
Arranged by JOSEPH DEVAUX

if you should ev - er wake, lis - ten to __ my song: "Sad is my

fate to have loved such a one as you. Why did I

wait, When I knew you could ne'er be true? So play on, gui-tar, __ for

tar-rung,   tar-rung,

me;   Play your plain - tive mel - o - dy."   tar - rung,   tar-

tar-rung.   *diminuendo*

rung.

diminuendo

pp

The Mermaid

Sea Chantey

Traditional

Arranged by MARSHALL BARTHOLOMEW

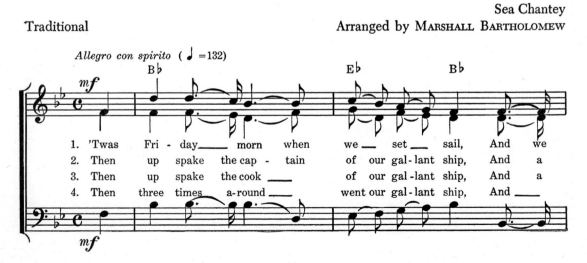

Allegro con spirito (♩ =132)

Bb   Eb   Bb

mf

1. 'Twas   Fri - day___   morn   when   we ___ set ___ sail,   And   we
2. Then   up   spake   the cap - tain   of   our gal -lant ship,   And   a
3. Then   up   spake   the cook ___   of   our gal -lant ship,   And   a
4. Then   three   times   a-round ___   went our gal -lant ship,   And ___

mf

44

were not— far from the land, When the cap-tain— spied— a
well-spo-ken man was — he; "I've mar-ried a wife— in
red hot— cook was — he; "I care much— more for my
three times a-round went— she, Then— three times a-round—

love-ly mer — maid With a comb and a glass in her hand.
Sa - lem— town, And to - night she a wid-dow will be."
ket-tles and my pots Than I do for the depths of the sea."
went our gal-lant ship, And she sank to the depths of the sea.

Refrain

p Oh, the o - cean waves may roll, And the storm-y winds— may—

blow While— we poor— sail-ors— go skip-ping to the tops And the
cresc.

may— blow—

accel. *a tempo*

land-lub-bers lie down be - low, be-low, be-low, And the land - lub-bers lie— down be - low.

45

Our Beautiful Valley

Brahms discovered this folk song in Suabia, a province of southern Germany, on one of his holidays. He deeply enjoyed the mountain scenery with its great rugged heights and deep shadowy valleys. The song is a genuine expression of these Suabian folk. Its essence was carefully preserved by Brahms in his arrangement. The accompaniment may be played effectively on either the guitar or the zither.

English version by
JULIA W. BINGHAM

German Folk Song
Arranged by JOHANNES BRAHMS

1. Our valley is beau-ti-ful, beau-ti-ful ev-er. In its shad-ows, dim shad-ows, we spoke of our love.
2. We knew that our love would last, last on for-ev-er, For the sun-shine, clear sun-shine, smiled down from a-bove.
3. For-got-ten the love we knew, knew such a short time, Yet I cher-ish, still cher-ish, that brief ec-sta-sy.
4. And wish you all hap-pi-ness, hap-pi-ness ev-er, With an-oth-er, that oth-er, who took you from me.

Birds' Winter Song

English version by
ELEANOR GRAHAM VANCE

SELIM PALMGREN

know us. Yet we have no time for griev-ing While we're grate-ful-

ly re-ceiv-ing Crumbs that thought-ful hands will throw us.

Selim Palmgren, born in Finland in 1878, is a contemporary composer known especially for his short piano pieces. In these he often uses folk music material, adding different harmonies and changing the melodies to create special descriptive effects. He has studied in Germany and Italy, and has played in concerts in Europe and the United States. He taught piano and composition in the Eastman School of Music in Rochester, N. Y.

Peter

English version by
ALFRED LITZERMAN

Russian Folk Song
Arranged by JOSEPH DeVAUX

Allegretto (♩ =138)

Ho, Heigh - ho, Heigh - ho, Heigh - ho.

Heigh - ho.

Heigh-ho, —— Heigh-ho, ho, Heigh - ho.

Swiss Evening Song

English version by
WALTER DUCLOUX

FERDINAND HUBERT
Arranged by WALTER DUCLOUX

1. Qui - et - ly eve - ning draws near.__ Hard - ly a
2. Si - lent and still lies the lake.__ But our good
1. Lue - gid vo Bärg__ ond Tal.__ Fliet scho de

mur - mur you hear.__ Down in the val - ley the shad -
Lord stays a - wake.__ Out of the night, while I'm sleep -
Son__ nesch - trahl__ Ond of de-n Aue-n__ ond Mat -

Don't You Go

Abbie Farwell Brown

Folk Song from Zamboanga
Arranged by Joseph DeVaux

Many Surprises *(Desprecio)*

English version by ELEANOR GRAHAM VANCE

Folk Song from Costa Rica
Piano accompaniment by FRED MENDELSOHN

Valse corrido (♩.=76)

mf

1. Life brings us many sur - pris - es,_____ No one can
2. Your heart be - longs to an - oth - er,_____ You say you
3. If a good fair - y could change you_____ In - to a

1. To - do su - ce - de en la vi - da_____ de lo que
2. Tu dic - es que ño me quie - res_____ por - que ya
3. Si fuen - te de a - gua te hi - cier - as_____ no ba - ja -

doubt this is true. _____ Fall - ing in love is a
can - not love me. _____ I, too, have some - one I'm
spring in the wood, _____ I would not drink of your

no hay que du - dar, _____ Que - da mi pren - da que
tiene s a qui - én _____ i - gual - i - tos es - tar
rí - a a be - ber, _____ aun - que de sed me mur -

trou - ble, _____ Pain - ful for me and for you. _____
lov - ing, _____ So we are ev - en, you see. _____
wa - ter, _____ For you would do me no good. _____

ri - da _____ he - cha un con - ti - nuo pe - nar.
e - mos _____ por - que yo ten - go tam - bién.
ier - a _____ por no vol - ver - te a que - rer.

The Minstrel Boy

Tom Moore, the Irish poet, wrote these new lines to be sung to an old Irish folk tune. The harpers used to sing to the soldiers in battle to encourage them to deeds of valor; but in this story the minstrel abandoned his harp for the sword. Many non-combatant troops have acted the same way in emergencies.

Irish Folk Song
Arranged by DANIEL DENNIS

THOMAS MOORE

wild harp_ slung____ be - hind____ him.
tore its_ chords____ a - sun - der;

wild harp slung_ be - hind him. "Land of song!" said the
tore its chords___ a - sun - der; And said, "No chain shall_

One sword, — at least,—
Thy songs __ were made__

war-rior bard, "Though all the world be - trays ___ thee, One sword, at least,_ thy
sul-ly thee, Thou soul of love and brav - er-y! Thy songs were made_for the

—— thy rights shall guard, One _ faith-ful _ harp___ shall praise _____ thee."
—— for pure and free, They shall nev - er_ sound__ in slav - 'ry."

rights shall guard, One_ faith-ful harp_ shall_ praise thee."
pure and free, They shall nev - er sound_ in_ slav - 'ry."

Friend of My Heart

English version by
ELEANOR GRAHAM VANCE

TISZA ALADÁR
Arranged by PER H. PETERSON

Friend of my heart, Turn — not a - way.

Why should we part When there's much to say?

Friend-ship's bonds will hold to - geth - er If on - ly we try. —
True com - pan - ions share their sor - row Straight through to the end. —

An - y trou - ble I can weath- er If you'll stand by.
Let us make a bright to - mor - row; Be my true friend.

Thrush Song

Clinton Scollard

Paul Hindemith

Hark to the song of the thrush, At the
List to the song of the thrush, From the

fall of the dusk and dew; Pierc - ing the twi - light—
shad - ows cool and deep, From the heart of the un - der-

hush,— Thrill - ing it through and through, While the first stars
brush— Where the pix - y peo - ple creep, While the winds grow

twin - kle, twin - kle, And the lit - tle leaves crin - kle, crin - kle,
crisp - er, crisp - er, And the lit - tle leaves whis - per, whis - per,

Low as a rill, clear as a bell, Down from the hill, up—
Fine as a flute blown at the morn, Soft as a lute, or—

from— the— dell, And— all for — me — and you!
fair - y — horn, A — call to the land— of sleep!

The Linden Tree

Schubert wrote six hundred songs in many moods. Some are long and dramatic, while others, like *The Linden Tree*, have the simple and expressive character of folk songs. Schubert's early experience as a choir boy taught him how to write well for voices.

English version by
JOHN TROUTBECK

FRANZ SCHUBERT

Beside the well and gate-way There stands a lin-den tree. Be-
But now I must have passed it Un-seen at dead of night; I

neath its friend-ly shad-ow What dreams have come to me. How
could not, in the dark-ness Once bring it in-to sight. Me-

oft up-on its branch-es I've carved a lov-ing word; What bursts of joy and
thought its branch-es whis-pered A call, to me ad-dressed, "Come here to me, my

sor-row The lin-den tree has heard; The lin-den tree has heard!
com-rade And find with me thy rest; And find with me thy rest."

61

Greensleeves

Arr. by Osbourne William McConathy
Piano accompaniment for unison singing by Howard Lindberg

English Folk Ballad

This song is not a traditional folk ballad, but was composed in the latter part of the 16th century. So popular did it become that Shakespeare refers to it in two of his plays. The modern English composer, Ralph Vaughan Williams, has arranged a beautiful setting of the tune for an interlude in the play, *Sir John in Love.*

FOLK AND NATIONAL DANCES

The Morris Dance is one of the most famous of the English folk dances. In England it is always a men's team dance and is performed with masculine vigor and enthusiasm. The costumes are most picturesque, and one effective feature is the row of bells fastened around the knees of each dancer. These tinkle with every movement.

In the United States the Morris Dance is ordinarily performed by both men's and women's teams, or by boys and girls. Here are directions for such an American adaptation. You may use the music for *Cornish May Song*, page 88. For dancing the tempo should be 160 instead of 126.

Formation: Teams of six boys or six girls (three on a side), all holding large white handkerchiefs, in parallel lines facing front of room. Each dancer should be about four feet away from the others.

Introduction: Stand in place, both arms forward, shoulder high		Counts 1, 2, 1, 2, 1, 2	3 measures
Last measure: Step forward, swinging arms down and back		Count 1	
Jump in air, landing on both feet, swinging arms forward and upward to position high over head		Count 2	1 measure
A. 1. Step forward left foot	Keeping arms straight, swing down and back	Count 1	
Step forward right foot		Count "and"	
Step forward left foot	Swing arms forward to	Count 2	
Hop on left foot	shoulder height	Count "and"	1 measure
2. Starting with right foot, repeat 1			1 measure
3. Step backward left foot	Raise hands over head and		
Hop on left foot	wave handkerchiefs in small circular movements	Count 1 "and"	
Step backward right foot	Continue waving	Count 2	
Hop on right foot		"and"	
Step backward left foot, knee bent	Swing arms down and back	Count 1	
Hold		"and"	
Jump, landing both feet	Swing arms up and forward	Count 2 "and"	2 measures

(Note: This section (A) comprises what is known as the Morris step.)

4. Repeat 1, 2, and 3, finishing with lines facing			4 measures
B. Moving to right, right hand over head			
1. a. Step sideward on ball of right foot, waving right hand in small circular movement		Count 1	
b. Close left foot to right		"and"	
2. Repeat 1		Count 2 "and"	1 measure
3. Repeat 1		Count 1 "and"	
4. Repeat 1-a (do not close left foot to right)		Count 2 "and"	1 measure
C. Moving to left, left hand over head, repeat all of B, finishing by closing right foot to left, weight on right foot			2 measures
D. Dancing the Morris Step (A), move forward and "cast off": Head of each line moves to rear of line; line follows, reversing position (head at foot, etc.)			4 measures
E. Repeat B, C, and D			8 measures
F. Repeat entire dance, using the music of the final ending to exit.			15 measures

The following directions may be used for a folk dance to go with *The Sierras of Chiapas*, page 36.

Formation: Facing front of room, girls form line, each girl two feet behind the girl in front of her. Boys form corresponding line four feet to left.

Introduction: Stand in place	2 measures

A. 1. a. Girls dance four step-brush-hops (step on right foot, brush toes of left foot forward, hop on right foot) toward boys, then return to place with the following step: — 2 measures

b. Step backward right foot	Count 1	
c. Lift left knee	Count 2	
d. Hop on right foot	Count 3	
e. Repeat b, c, and d, starting on left foot	Counts 4, 5, 6	1 measure
f. Repeat b, c, d, and e		1 measure
2. a. Boys dance toward girls and		
b. back, as in 1		4 measures
B. Repeat A, facing front at finish of step		8 measures

C. Head of each line "casts off" (see directions for the Morris Dance on preceding page), dancing to rear of line, turning in, and returning to original position, using this step:

1. Six short running steps, starting with right foot	Counts 1 to 6	1 measure
2. Step-brush-hop right	Counts 1, 2, 3	
Repeat to left	Counts 4, 5, 6	1 measure
3. Repeat 1 and 2 three times, ending with two lines facing		6 measures

D. Repeat A, with this change: as the boys' line meets the girls' line, boys and girls grasp hands. As boys move backward, girls move with them. — 8 measures

Many dances are definitely national in character. *The Dancing Maiden*, page 40, may be sung while the Swedish *Hambo* is danced. Another very typical national dance is the *Jutlandish Dance Song*, page 66.

Formation: Groups of partners stand in rows, hands on hips.

A. 1. Each dancer steps right on right foot	Count 1	
2. Close left foot to right, weight on left foot	Count 2	1 measure
3. Repeat 1 and 2 three times		3 measures
4. Repeat four times to left		4 measures
B. Taking right hands and holding them high, partners dance eight skips clockwise around each other		4 measures
C. Repeat A, twice (not four times) to right, twice to left, and finish facing each other		4 measures
D. In ballroom dance position, partners dance eight box-waltz steps around room. (One box-waltz step: boy takes one waltz step forward, starting left foot, then one waltz step backward; girl waltzes one step backward, starting right foot, then one step forward)		8 measures
E. Repeat A, B, C, and D. (Partners may change after each verse.)		24 measures

Jutlandish Dance Song

English version by
ELEANOR SMITH

Danish Folk Song
Arranged by HEINRICH REIMANN

Oh Lord So Wondrous

English version by
Julia W. Bingham

Edvard Grieg
Arranged by Per H. Peterson

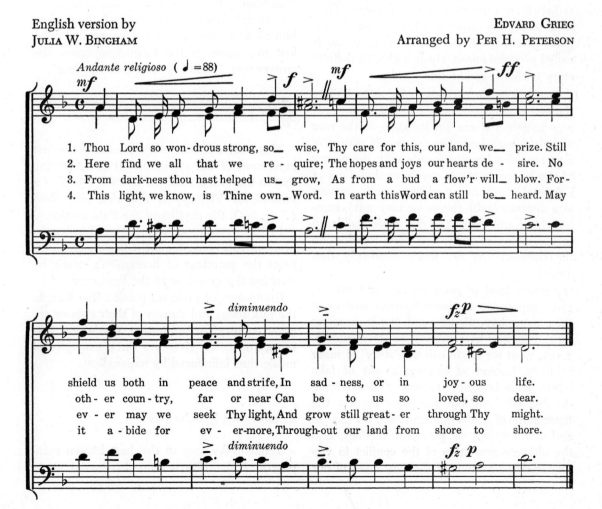

1. Thou Lord so won-drous strong, so_ wise, Thy care for this, our land, we_ prize. Still
2. Here find we all that we re-quire; The hopes and joys our hearts de-sire. No
3. From dark-ness thou hast helped us_ grow, As from a bud a flow'r will_ blow. For-
4. This light, we know, is Thine own_ Word. In earth this Word can still be_ heard. May

shield us both in peace and strife, In sad-ness, or in joy-ous life.
oth-er coun-try, far or near Can be to us so loved, so dear.
ev-er may we seek Thy light, And grow still great-er through Thy might.
it a-bide for ev-er-more, Through-out our land from shore to shore.

Why do we love music? Why do we want to listen to it?

It has been said that music states feelings and emotions that are too deep for words. Where words leave off, music begins. The composer tries to express joy, sorrow, peace, tragedy, comedy, humor, dignity, frivolity, and other feelings that people have. We are aware of these things when we listen to music.

Music may also attract us because of its fascinating rhythm, its beautiful melody, the richness of its harmony, and the appealing tone quality of the instruments upon which it is played.

To some composers, form and method seem more important than the message. In the 18th century it was the custom to write in so-called sonata form, but in the 19th century, composers began to write short pieces which told stories rather than expressed abstract ideas. They tried to express in music what a story or program meant to them. This kind of music is called *program music*. Music without a definite story is known as *absolute music*.

Program music may go so far as to imitate the actual sounds of nature to tell its story. It may imitate a storm, for instance, or the roar of battle, with booming cannon. It may give a picture of a horseback ride with the clatter of the horse's hoofs. It may give the effect of a funeral march or a wedding march, starting at a distance (with the music very soft), coming closer and closer (as the music builds up to a crashing climax), and then receding in the distance (as the music gradually dies away).

Another kind of program music, however, gives expression to inner feelings and emotions, as we have already said. But it expresses these emotions as a growth or development, giving what we might call the "story" of inner conflicts. Instead of hearing a sort of fake battle with booming cannon and charging cavalry, we hear the composer express the inner battle of conflicting emotions, the change and development of powerful feelings, and the ultimate resolution of the conflict in victory or despair. Some of the very finest of our music may be said to have this sort of "program."

Between program and absolute music, there are many compositions that have elements of both kinds of music. There is no sharp dividing line. But if you learn to distinguish these elements in the music you hear, you will have a clearer understanding of it, and more pleasure in listening.

Beethoven, Symphony No. 5 in C Minor

In his *Symphony No. 5, in C minor,* the great composer, Ludwig van Beethoven, used the 18th century sonata form (a symphony is a sonata for full orchestra) to express his innermost thoughts.

One authority, Robert Schauffler, sees in the symphony's four movements the composer's "emotional struggle to victory." Beethoven himself was once asked what he meant by the first movement of the Fifth Symphony. His answer was, "Thus fate knocks at the door":

This motive of four notes dominates the first movement of the symphony. It is interesting that in the Morse code the letter V (used as a symbol for Victory) is *dot, dot, dot, dash* (. . . —), the rhythm of the Fate motive.

In the painting reproduced as the frontispiece of this book, the artist has aimed to express the grandeur of Beethoven's music by showing the grandeur of the landscape.

Composers of program music often turn to the folk songs and dances of their own or another country for inspiration, rhythmical patterns, and color. Here are three examples of music thus influenced by nationalism.

Tchaikovsky, Marche Slav

Tchaikovsky, one of the best known composers of the 19th century in Russia, wrote symphonies, operas, symphonic poems (program music), and ballets. In his *Marche Slav*, Tchaikovsky used the Russian national hymn, as well as several folk tunes. A melody from the *Marche Slav*, based on a characteristic Serbian love song, follows:

Liszt, Hungarian Rhapsody No. 14

Liszt, one of the greatest pianists of the 19th century, was an outstanding figure in music because of his interesting experiments in composition. Among the most original and important of his many works are his nineteen *Hungarian Rhapsodies*.

Liszt left his native Hungary as a child prodigy, but when he visited it later as a great pianist, the music of the Gypsies attracted him. No one knows where the Gypsies came from, but members of this wandering tribe roved throughout Central Europe and made music wherever they went. They wrote no music down, but improvised on folk tunes of different countries as they played their fiddles and cembalos, instruments with metal strings which are played with small hammers.

The best-loved dance of the Gypsies was the Hungarian *czardas* (char'-das) with its two contrasting parts, *lassan*, which is slow and sad, and *friska*, which is fast and fiery. Liszt used these rhythms in his Rhapsodies, sometimes composing tunes to sound like Gypsy music, but often using the real melodies.

Two themes from *Rhapsody, No. 14, lassan* and *friska* follow:

The painting on page 30 by Robert Riggs, has captured the spirit of this exciting music.

Falla, The Three-Cornered Hat

The most famous Spanish composer of the 20th century was Manuel de Falla. He searched deeply into the heart of his native land and tried to put what he found there into his music. *The Three-Cornered Hat** is a ballet on a humorous story originally called *The Corregidor and the Miller's Wife*. In it Falla quoted a few folk tunes, wrote original music on familiar rhythms, and used the effect of Spain's most popular instrument, the guitar.

Three dances from *The Three-Cornered Hat* are frequently played in concert programs. The first, *The Neighbors*, opens with this melody:

In the second work, *The Miller's Dance*, Falla used rhythms which are very typical of Spanish music. For example:

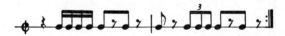

In the final dance, Falla used the well-known tune and rhythm of the "Jota" as a basis for his own music:

*Copyright by J. & W. Chester, Ltd., London.

69

Vangeline

English version by
ELEANOR GRAHAM VANCE

Greek Folk Song
Arranged by JAMES ALIFERIS

Gracefully (♪ =132)

Mm — Mm —

1. Oh, who art thou, La - dy
2. The cy - press tree and the
3. The wa - ter thou bring-est

Mm — Mm — Mm

Van - ge-line? Thou rul - est here like a love - ly queen. Oh, love - ly queen.
lem - on tree. Hold up their boughs for a drink from thee. The drink from thee.
from the sky Must quench their thirst or the trees will die. The trees will die.

Mm

From the sky thou dost ap - pear, Bring-ing bless - ed wa - ter so pure and clear; Oh—
Fail them not, Oh love - ly one. Leave them not to burn in the sum - mer sun. The—
Mer - cy, mer - cy, La - dy mine, Let thy rain-drops fall on the tree and vine. The—

Mm

who art thou, La - dy Van - ge-line? Thou rul - est here like a love - ly queen.
cy-press tree and the lem - on tree Hold up their boughs for a drink from thee.
wa - ter thou bring-est from the sky Must quench their thirst or the trees will die.

Mm

70

Seguidilla from La Mancha

The Seguidilla is a dance song originating in the hot, dry country of southeastern Spain. It is traditionally played by guitars and castanets, and its tempo is rather fast. The musicians usually sing as they play, and the dancers handle the castanets. In the opera *Carmen*, there is a Seguidilla which Carmen sings to José.

Spanish Folk Song
Arranged by LEONHARD DEUTSCH

WILLARD R. TRASK

our Man - za - nar - es, _____ Where life is gay and free! _____
long may I _____ sing them! _____ Long may their ech - oes ring! _____

Long live La Man - cha! Long live my ___ girl! Long live my
Long live La Man - cha! Long live my ___ girl! Long live my

girl with jet - black ___ eyes! Long live my girl with jet - black ___ eyes!
girl with jet - black ___ eyes! Long live my girl with jet - black ___ eyes!

3. There's on - ly one for ___ me. One ___ bright ___ girl, one ___ right ___

girl. Black her eyes are, she loves me tru-ly,

Our love is dear to me. Long live La Man-cha!

Long live my girl! Long live my girl with jet-black eyes! Long live my

girl with jet-black eyes!

The Castle Tower

English version by
ANN MACMILLAN

Czech Folk Song
Arranged by ANN MACMILLAN

Moderato (♩ =132)

mf A - bove the field of green and gold A young lad's head you
But look a - gain. It's not a head, But If - ca's cas - tle

(Melody)

mf A - bove the field of green and gold A young lad's head you
But look a - gain. It's not a head, But If - ca's cas - tle

now be - hold. *p* A - hu - ya, hu - ya, hu - ya - ya, Fast and flow-ing riv - er. A-
tower in - stead.

now be - hold. *p* A - hu - ya, hu - ya, hu - ya - ya, Fast and flow-ing riv - er. A-
tower in - stead.

hu - ya, hu - ya, hu - ya - ya, Fast flow-ing riv - er.

hu - ya, hu - ya, hu - ya - ya, Fast and flow-ing riv - er.

74

All Through the Night

The Welsh people are noted for their love of music, especially singing. Every town has its choral society, and every year there is a national musical and literary festival, where prizes are awarded to singers, poets, and composers. The arranger was the elder brother of Walter Damrosch.

Sir Harold Boulton

Welsh Folk Song
Arranged by Frank Damrosch

Waltzing Matilda

Marie Cowan
Arranged by Howard Lindberg

A. B. Patterson

Waltz - ing Ma - til - da, waltz - ing Ma - til - da, You'll come a - waltz - ing Ma -

til - da, with me. {And he sang as he sat and waited by the bil - la - bong,}
{And he sang as he talked to that jum - buck in his tuck - er - bag.}

"You'll come a - waltz - ing, Ma - til - da, with me."

3. Down came the stockman, riding on his thoroughbred,
   Down came the troopers, one, two, three.
   "Where's the jolly jumbuck you've got in your tuckerbag?
   You'll come a-waltzing, Matilda, with me."

4. Up jumped the swagman and plunged into the billabong,
   "You'll never catch me alive," cried he,
   And his ghost may be heard as you ride beside the billabong,
   "You'll come a-waltzing, Matilda, with me."

Swagman — a tramp   Jumbuck — a sheep   Tuckerbag — a knapsack

Billabong — a water hole in a dry river bed   Coolibah tree — an eucalyptus

Far-Away Valley

English version by
ANN MACMILLAN

Finnish Folk Song
Arranged by MARSHALL BARTHOLOMEW

Far, far a - way is a green, roll - ing val - ley

Fair - er, by far, than a king's gold - en hall.___ Oh, lit - tle bird, is___

that where you're go - ing?__ Take me there with you! Take me as I call!

Take me there with you!__ Take me as I call!

Serenade in Vain

Wendish Folk Song
Arranged by Leonhard Deutsch

Willard R. Trask

"Are you sleep-ing,   are   you wak - ing? Your poor Yan - ek's   heart is__ break - ing.__
I may love just   whom I want__ to,   On - ly one thing   that I __ can't__ do: __
Now it's real - ly   light.   I won - der Who's that wom- an   com-ing__ yon - der? __

Find some way   to   me to__ creep,   Now__ your__ moth- er's__   fast a - sleep."
'Nev - er leave your   room,' she__ said,   'When__ the__ sun__ has__   gone to bed.' "
Bless me, it's   my   moth - er!" 'Quick!   Yan-ek, bet-ter run or you will taste her stick!"

Vidalita

English version by
IRMA LABASTILLE

Uruguayan Folk Song

Andantino (♩ =96)

p

rit.

A-Roving

In the old days of sailing vessels, many of the chores now done by machines were done by hand. To lighten their work and to give rhythm to their efforts, the sailors sang work-songs called *chanties* (pronounced "shanties"). Often, these songs took the form of a ballad that told a story, and sometimes assumed an international aspect as the ballads were passed from the sailors of one country to the sailors of another country.

Sea Chantey

Traditional

Arranged by MARSHALL BARTHOLOMEW

Hatikvah (The Hope)

Hebrew words by N. IMBER
English version by RABBI JACOB FREEDMAN

Traditional Melody
Arranged by S. G. BRASLAVSKY

Prom-ised Land of Zi - on, Where he - roes lived and died!
Kol od ba - ley - vav, pni - mah,

Mar - tyred, Thy chil - dren, Stir with hope and pride! From
Ne - fesh ye - hu - di ho - mi - ya! Ul'-

dis - tant lands of ex - ile To bless - ed East - ern shore,
fa - tey Miz - rah Ka - di - ma,

84

Hatikvah was written about 1878 as a Hebrew poem, by Naphtali Herz Imber. The music is based upon a melody in the *Sefardi* (Spanish-Portuguese Jewish) Festival liturgy and was set to words some years later. In 1948 Hatikvah was officially adopted as the Israeli national anthem.

*New refrain — as sung in Israel

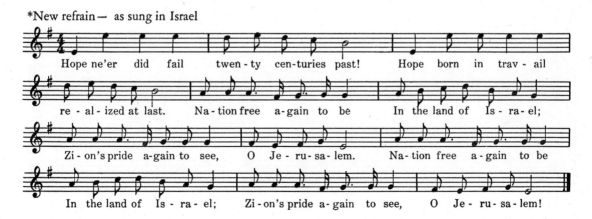

One Quiet Night

Brahms, the son of a bass viol player, spent an unhappy childhood in Altova, a suburb of Hamburg. But when he was a man he remembered with pleasure the folk songs he had heard as a child and he made a collection of them. He dedicated these songs to the children of his friends, —Robert and Clara Schumann. He later arranged some of these folk songs for mixed voices.

English version by
AILEEN FISHER

German Folk Song
Arranged by JOHANNES BRAHMS

One qui - et night be - fore the light, I heard a sad voice sing - ing, Up on the breeze that stirred the trees The tear - ful sound was cling - ing. It tore a - part my list'- ning heart And made me weep with sor - row, And flow'rs be - low had tears to show For dew up - on the mor - row.

SINGING NOTES

Most of you have probably heard the *Hungarian Dances,* Numbers 5 and 6, by Johannes Brahms, for they are played often in concerts and on the radio. In these dances, as in many of his other compositions, Brahms used the melodies of folk songs and dances as his themes.

The song *One Quiet Night* is a good illustration of this usage. The melody is an old Suabian folk tune. But Brahms' beautiful harmonization almost converts this simple melody into an art song.

An art song, as you may know, is a poem set to music by a known composer. The melody and harmony enhance the beauty and meaning of the poem, and the accompaniment often gives depth and forcefulness to the mood of the words. You will appreciate this quality of the art song if you have ever listened to *The Erlking,* by Franz Schubert.

A folk song, on the other hand, is a song that has been handed down from generation to generation, sometimes without ever having been written down. The composer is usually unknown, and frequently many versions of the song exist. The words were made up by the first person who sang it, and as it was handed down, the text and even the tune were changed to suit the singer. A folk song usually describes some activity or event, speaks of love of home and country, or describes the sentiments of a suitor for his lady. Many are in dance rhythm and were used for both singing and dancing.

Often it is possible right at the start to sing a melody in a very natural, pleasing way. But as you begin to learn more about what music can really express, you will want to get more variety and meaning in your singing. Then you must take care not to lose any naturalness or freedom in using your voice while you are thinking about giving more force and feeling to your songs.

Naturalness is a difficult thing to keep, strange as it may seem. Many people, as they grow older, get high-pitched, strained voices, even in speaking. This is one thing that singing, the right kind of singing, can help. When you take care to make your singing beautiful in sound, you will also be helping to make your speaking voice beautiful.

There is more to singing, however, than keeping a beautiful tone of voice. In really fine songs, the composer has made the music suit the words, and one should follow the composer's intention of bringing out the sense of the words.

One Quiet Night, page 86, is a delightful song to sing, not only because of the beauty of the melody and harmony, but also because of its fine adaptability to voices. Notice the smoothness of the melody, which moves so naturally from tone to tone. Notice too, the simple and easy phrasing which so effectively interprets the meaning of the text.

In achieving beautiful singing and fine interpretation of this song, you must apply your skill and knowledge of good voice production. Tone quality may be improved by singing the entire song in unison on the syllable "ah." Feel that your voice flows over the notes without any break whatsoever, and think of the meaning of the words and express it in the quality of your voice. Phrase exactly as though you were singing the words. Then sing again on "ah," but this time in parts, again phrasing as though using the words. Now try to keep the same even tone quality and smooth phrasing while you sing the words. As you sing be sure that your breath support is properly maintained, your throat feels comfortable, your posture is good, and that you make the words clear by pronouncing very accurately.

Your final interpretation of the song should reflect the quiet mood which Brahms has created with this simple folk-melody. The movement, "rather slowly," and the atmosphere of the text indicate that you should begin rather softly *(p).* But the three-beat rhythm suggests an easy swing without lagging. The melodic and harmonic climax occurs on the line "and made me weep with sorrow." After that, you will feel like singing more and more quietly to the end. Try several interpretations, and then decide which you like best. Having solo singers sing the words and melody, while the others hum the harmony, is very effective, and makes this an excellent song for concert use.

Cornish May Song

English Folk Song
Arranged by FRED MENDELSOHN

SIR ALEXANDER BOSWELL

Moderato (♩ =132)

Ye maids of_ Hel-ston_gath-er dew While_ yet the morn-ing_ breez-es blow; The
Though a - ges_ close and_ man - ners fade, And_ an - cient rev-els_ pass a - way; In

Gath - er_ dew While_ yet_ the morn-ing_ breez-es blow;
Man - ners_fade, And_ an - cient rev - els_ pass a - way;

fair - y_ rings are_ fresh and new, Then _ cau - tious mark_them_
Hel - ston_ let it _ not be said, For - got - ten is_ sweet_

Fair - y rings are fresh and new, Then cau - tious mark them_
Hel - ston let it not be said, For - got - ten is sweet_

as ye go.
Flo - ra Day. A - rise, a - rise, a - wake to joy, The sky - lark hails the

dawn of day; Care, get thee hence, from Hel - ston fly! For mirth rules here this

morn of May. morn of May. For mirth rules here this morn of May.

89

Man discovered many centuries ago that sound could be produced by blowing into a hollow object. The same principle is used today in playing a wind instrument. The earliest of these, if they could be called instruments, undoubtedly were very crude — sea shells, animal horns, or hollow reeds. It is a far cry from these early beginnings to the smooth wind instruments of today, but the basic method of producing sound by blowing is the same.

Wind instruments are divided into two families, "woodwinds" and "brass." The tone quality of each is very distinct, but the basis of the division is sometimes confusing because some instruments of the woodwind type are actually made of metal.

The woodwind family includes the flute, oboe, clarinet, and bassoon. The flute has a little companion called the piccolo, which is actually a small flute. The oboe has a companion in the English horn, which is not actually a horn but an alto oboe, larger and lower in pitch than the regular oboe. Most clarinets used today are B-flat clarinets; A clarinets, which provide simpler fingering for selections written in certain keys, are also in use. Symphony orchestras from time to time use a bass clarinet, and bands employ alto clarinets and small E-flat clarinets. The bassoon, which is the woodwind instrument with the lowest pitch, has a companion, the contra-bassoon that plays an octave lower. Between the highest notes of the piccolo and the lowest tones of the contra-bassoon there is an enormous pitch range that compares roughly with the range of the piano.

In the previous chapter we spoke of the string section of a symphony orchestra. The second section is composed of the members of the woodwind family. Each instrument has its own very special tone quality, but if it is played for very long periods it tends to tire the listener. Composers, therefore, are usually careful to use the woodwinds mainly for certain color effects and to rely on the strings for the foundation of the music. Occasional passages, of course, are given entirely to the wood-winds, and they can sometimes be quite effective as solo instruments if used skillfully.

The brass family includes the trumpet, cornet, French horn, trombone, baritone horn, and tuba. The cornet and the trumpet are much alike, but the trumpet has a brilliant, martial tone, while the quality of the cornet is softer, less brilliant, and more suited to playing ballads and song melodies. Trumpets, French horns, trombones, and tubas are used in concert orchestras. These same instruments are used in bands together with cornets, mellophones, and baritone horns.

Actually, the brass section, the third section of a symphony orchestra, consists of trumpets, trombones, tubas and French horns. Sometimes the trumpets and trombones are referred to as the "heavy artillery" of the orchestra. This is because they are used frequently to create great climaxes when much sound is wanted, but they are also valuable for solo work and soft passages. Trombones, for example, can be used to express majesty and grandeur. Trumpets are very effective in passages that have a military character, and are also used in other passages to give brilliance and excitement to the music. However, each instrument can also be used in passages having a quiet, song-like effect.

The tuba supplies the lowest part, and occasionally it is used for comical effects. The French horn is somewhat similar in tone quality to the woodwinds and it blends especially well with them. As a solo instrument the French horn is superb.

Since the days of Mozart, Haydn, and Beethoven, composers have taken advantage of the unusual musical effects obtained by using the French horn in combination with woodwind instruments, and many important chamber works have resulted. (See page 210 for a discussion of chamber music).

All the instruments, woodwind, brass, and string, have individual qualities and characteristics. When you listen to orchestral music, you will find it interesting to try to identify the individual instruments that form the many musical sounds that come over your radio and record player.

Five Rounds

Composers Unknown

The rays of ear - ly morn - ing Now gleam on hill and field;
And flow'rs the plain a - dorn - ing Their pleas - ant fra - grance yield.

Fare -well, dear; peace be with thee; When I'm gone, then___ think of me.

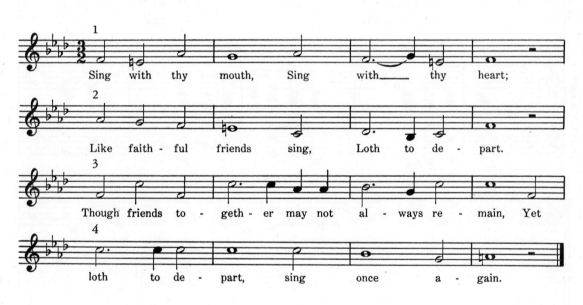

Sing with thy mouth, Sing with___ thy heart;
Like faith - ful friends sing, Loth to de - part.
Though friends to - geth - er may not al - ways re - main, Yet
loth to de - part, sing once a - gain.

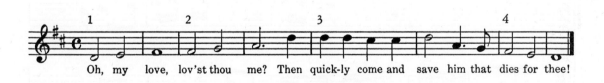

Oh, my love, lov'st thou me? Then quick-ly come and save him that dies for thee!

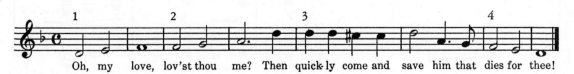

Oh, my love, lov'st thou me? Then quick-ly come and save him that dies for thee!

Rantin' Rovin' Robin

Scotch Folk Song
Arranged by Marshall Bartholomew

Robert Burns

Few people in Scotland now speak Gaelic, the original language of the northern part. In the eastern counties we find many reminders of the Scandinavians who raided the coast in bygone days, such as *bairn* for "child." In the southern counties, "the lowlands," various dialects of English are spoken. Many of Burns' poems are in Ayrshire dialect.

Some of the interesting expressions in this dialect follow: A *gossip* is a fortune-teller, who *peek't* (peered) into his *loof* (the palm of his hand). This *waly* (big) boy is no *coof* (fool).

The tune of this song is much older than the words. The sixteenth notes should be sung on true pitch at the speed of the song, just as a flute or a clarinet would play it.

Moo-Lee-Hua

English version by
ANN MACMILLAN

Chinese Folk Song
Piano accompaniment by WALTER KOB

Moderato (♩=84)

I know a gar-den_ bright as_ day

Where Moo-Leeflow'rs_in_ white ar-ray Stand, re-flect-ing_ sun-light's glare,

Giv-ing_ fra-grance_ to the_ air. Brief_are their lives and quick-ly_ done;

Yet they_try_to_ shine More_ bright-ly than_the_ sun.

Music in These United States

I hear America singing, the varied carols I
    hear,
Those of mechanics, each one singing his, as
    it should be, blithe and strong,
The carpenter singing his, as he measures his
    plank or beam,
The mason singing his, as he makes ready
    for work, or leaves off work,
The boatman singing what belongs to him
    in his boat, the deckhand singing on the
    steamboat deck,
The shoemaker singing as he sits on his
    bench, the hatter singing as he stands,
The wood-cutter's song, the ploughboy's on
    his way in the morning, or at the noon
    intermission, or at sundown,
The delicious singing of the mother, or of
    the young wife at work, or of the girl
    sewing or washing,
Each singing what belongs to him or her
    and to none else,
The day what belongs to the day — at night
    the party of young fellows, robust,
    friendly,
Singing, with open mouths their strong
    melodious songs.

Although Walt Whitman, one of our great
poets, wrote this stirring tribute to America
nearly a hundred years ago, what he said is, in
a large measure, just as true today. The singing
that Whitman heard and wrote about was a
wonderful kind of singing — where the singer
sang, not for personal acclaim and applause,
but for the sheer joy of singing. Sometimes the
composers of the songs were known, but usually not. The composer was not important! The
important thing was that the songs were dearly
loved and were sung from memory. Today we
call this kind of song a "folk song" — song of
the people.

We have much folk music in the United
States. Some of it is very old, going back as far
as the Revolutionary War and earlier, and some
of it is almost current. This music is as varied
as America is big and great. We have Indian
songs, cowboy songs, lumberjack songs, sea
chanteys, work songs, dance songs, songs about
famous and mythical characters, religious
songs, and many others.

Along with folk music, there was trans-
planted to this country a kind of music that is
studied and written down according to more
or less definite rules of composition. At first this
music, which we call *art* music, was limited to
the larger seaboard cities, but gradually it
began to spread as foreign-trained musicians
migrated to America.

The first known American-born composer of
art music was Francis Hopkinson, a signer of
the Declaration of Independence and a friend
of George Washington. His music, written in
the style of European music of that day, was
considered quite good. *My Love Is Gone to
Sea*, page 100, is a good example of his compositions and an interesting song to sing.
Another early American composer, William
Billings, was more original in his writings;
although it is crude, his music suggests something of the vigor and spirit of his age. *Putney
Hymn*, page 102, is one of his more appealing
songs. Edward MacDowell, who was the first
American composer to gain wide recognition
abroad, and who is considered by many to be
our greatest composer, died early in this
century.

For the past quarter-century, people's music
(which includes current popular music) and
art music have thrived side by side, and have
influenced each other. Some composers of art
music have drawn on the popular for rhythms,
types and styles of melody, and orchestration.
Among this group are men like Aaron Copland,
and even foreign-born composers such as
Milhaud and Hindemith. On the other hand,
William Grant Still, George Gershwin, and
others have written serious art music.

Joseph Pickett, an American artist renowned
for his straightforward style, painted "Manchester Valley," which is reproduced on the
following page. Note the fresh charm of this
vivid impression of an American scene.

The briefest description of American music
would not be complete without recognizing
the unique place of Stephen Foster. He wrote
music that the people took up and eagerly
made their own. And today some of his songs
are known throughout the world.

"Manchester Valley" by JOSEPH PICKETT. From the Museum of Modern Art.

Ute Mountain Air

Ute Tribal Air
Arranged by Roy E. Freeburg

97

I Ride an Old Paint

Cowboy Ballad

Arranged by JOSEPH DeVAUX

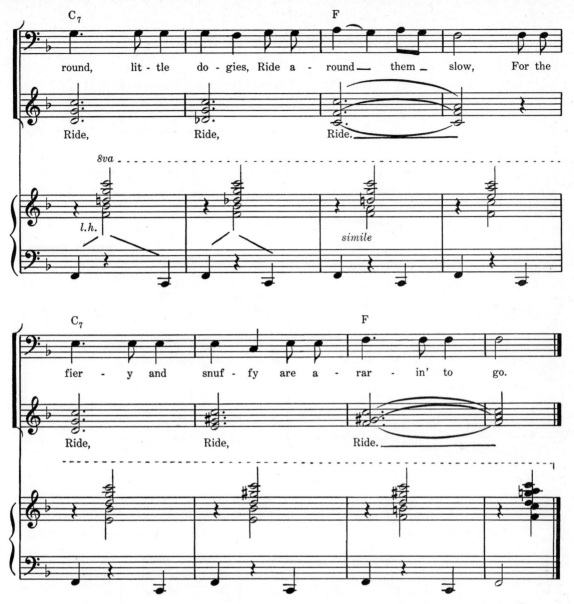

The melody of *I Ride an Old Paint,* instead of being in the soprano part as most melodies are, is in the lowest part, and it is written in the bass clef. This clef works just like the treble clef except that it is thirteen notes lower in pitch. Usually, the bass clef is used for voices and instruments whose ranges are so low that if the treble were used, most of the notes would be on leger lines. If for example, we used the treble clef for this song, it would begin like this:

As you can see, it would be difficult to read such a low part in the treble clef.

Let's compare the same *F* Major scale as it is written on both the treble and bass staves:

When piano accompaniments have low notes for the right hand, you will sometimes see them written with a bass clef on what is usually the treble staff. For the same reason, high notes for the left hand are written with a treble clef on what would usually be the bass staff. This avoids the extensive use of leger lines.

99

My Love Is Gone to Sea

This song is very typical of the period in history when it was written. It
was published in 1788.

FRANCIS HOPKINSON
Piano accompaniment by WALTER KOB

My_ love is gone to sea Whilst_ I his ab-sence mourn,_ No_

joy shall smile on me_____ Un - til my love_ re - turn.____ He_

Francis Hopkinson, born in Philadelphia in 1737, was a many-sided man — a lawyer, judge, statesman, poet, and musician. He was one of the signers of the Declaration of Independence, and may be called the first American composer. This song is one of a group dedicated to George Washington.

The Putney Hymn

Billings, born in Boston in 1746, was a pioneer music teacher and choral conductor. Although self-taught, the vigor of his songs made them popular in his time. His hymn, "Chester," reflects his ardent patriotism, and became in New England the battlecry of the army of the American Revolution. Putney was a town where Billings held one of his singing classes.

WILLIAM BILLINGS

WILLIAM BILLINGS   Piano accompaniment by LEONHARD DEUTSCH

DANCE PATTERNS

When form in music was discussed on page 17, you will remember reading how a work of art is planned. The same thing is true of the dance, and dances are made up of patterns and patterns within patterns. Furthermore, patterns of dance and patterns of music are alike. This relationship is made particularly clear by directional marching and in country dancing. In both cases the divisions of the music determine the pattern developed. In country ("square") dancing, each new section of the music calls for change, either in spirit, step, figure, or direction. These changes form the design or floor pattern.

If you are not familiar with the planning of floor patterns, you will enjoy commencing with one of the simplest forms, the round. On page 91 there are several rounds from which to choose. They are four-part rounds, so divide your group into four parts. Each group should perform the same movements, but should begin in sequence, as each voice enters when the round is sung. The base pattern might be: step forward (one step to every one or two beats) first phrase, step backward second phrase. Thus the second group moves forward as the first steps backward, and the third moves forward as the second steps backward, and so on. This pattern may have many variations, which will come to you as you gain experience.

Along with the planning of floor patterns (the design made by the feet as they move on a flat surface) is another very intriguing rhythmic activity—the study of an arrangement of a tune or the analysis of the structure of a piece of music as it might relate to a formalized dance. The technical name for this is *choreography*. For example, try to plan the possible choreography for the *Ute Mountain Air* on page 97. The following suggestions may be helpful:

Boys — study the third voice part, music and words. Notice the steady four-beat movement, suggesting a very masculine foot pattern. What kind of step would an Indian use?

Girls — study the two upper parts. Does the music suggest rhythmic movement? Try dividing the girls into two groups to correspond to soprano and alto voices. Let partners plan movements to follow the rhythm pattern of each part. When the two parts sing in unison, move together. When the parts divide, indicate the division. One way to do this is to face in opposite directions, or to reverse arm movements. You will find it exciting to see your dance pattern grow.

You have beaten time or conducted in twos, threes, and fours. *Vangeline* (page 70), a Greek folk melody, is written in an unusual rhythm of seven beats to a measure. It will help you to feel this rhythm and sing the song in time if you keep time with arm movements. Start with the right hand held high. On count 1, bring arm down in front of body at waist level; count 2, swing the right arm out to the side; count 3, raise to starting position; count 4, drop arm to front; count 5, raise again; count 6, down; count 7, up to starting position. Notice that you have divided the measure into three parts—first, three beats, then two, then two more. The three-beat pattern matches the dotted-quarter notes, and the two groups of two-beats match the two quarter notes that complete each measure. Can you make up a foot movement in the same plan?

Mike Fink (page 112) contains many ideas for another dance form. Mike Fink was champion of the race of rivermen who propelled the keelboats that carried freight up and down the river, before the day of steamboats. He wore a red feather, meaning that he called the orders on his boat. In your pantomime, one boy may impersonate the man who steered the boat, from the stern. This steersman moves the tiller from side to side (one swing to a measure). Other boys impersonate polemen standing on either side of the boat, who work vigorously to get the boat in midstream and afloat down river, with only two men rowing. At the start, pole hard (one thrust to a measure). Later, the polemen relax and dance to the tune of the fiddler who plays a jig, in the center of the boat. (His violin bow moves two swings to a measure.)

Between the second and third stanzas, the boat is unloaded in New Orleans. Girls meet the boatmen and there is couple dancing (third stanza). The poling begins again while the chorus is sung.

Climbin' Up the Mountain

Negro Spiritual
Arranged by JOSEPH DeVAUX

Climb - in' up the moun - tain, chil - dren, ___ I did-n't come here for to stay. ___ If I nev - er - more see you a - gain, ___ I'll meet you on the judg-ment day, Good Lord, ___ I'll meet you on the judg-ment day!

Gould, Cowboy Rhapsody

When great herds of cattle were driven across the plains from Texas to the Western markets (1870-1890), they were accompanied by the cowboys who sang, whistled, and made up new verses to old tunes to pass the time as they rode the long trail.

These cowboy songs are true folk music, and *The Old Chisholm Trail* was one of the most popular. It is used by the American composer, Morton Gould, in his orchestral work, *Cowboy Rhapsody.** Many versions of this tune exist. Mr. Gould uses it as follows:

He uses another famous cowboy song, *Home on the Range,* with different instruments, such as the bassoon and the English horn.

Morton Gould's first-hand experience with jazz and his interest in folk music form the basis of his composing. He says that one of his chief aims is "to fuse the elements of our popular American idioms with the classical form and structure."

MacDowell, A. D. 1620

The true spirit of romanticism is embodied in the work of Edward MacDowell, who is without question the best known and most loved American composer of the 19th century.

MacDowell, a native New Yorker, studied with many teachers, among them the famous South American pianist, Teresa Carreno. At fifteen he studied in Paris, and later in Frankfort, intending to become a concert pianist. After his return to America, he lived in Boston. In 1896 he was made head of the newly founded music department of Columbia University. He resigned from that position in 1904, just four years before his death.

In one of his *Sea Pieces, Op. 55, No. 3, A. D. 1620,*† MacDowell celebrated the arrival of the Puritan settlers in New England. As a true romanticist, he combined poetry and painting with his musical ideas. A picture called "The Golden Galleon" may have inspired the poem that prefaces the piece:

> *The yellow setting sun*
> *   Melts the lazy sea to gold*
> *And gilds the swaying galleon*
> *   That towards a land of promise*
> *Lunges hugely on.*

The music pictures the galleon in a march-like movement, like this:

The hymn-like middle section reminds one of our well-known song, *America:*

In 1920, when the 300th anniversary of the coming of the Pilgrims was celebrated at Plymouth, Massachusetts, MacDowell's *A. D. 1620* was played in an orchestral version, and words were added to the middle section, which was sung as a hymn.

*Copyright Mills Music, Inc. Used by permission.

†Copyright 1898 by P. L. JUNG. Copyright Renewed. By permission of THE ARTHUR P. SCHMIDT CO., INC.

PERCUSSION INSTRUMENTS

Those who have studied early music and the music of primitive peoples tell us that man first produced sound by striking, slapping, pounding, and shaking objects; that is, by percussion. They also tell us that the first musical instruments were drums. Today, familiar as we are with the modern percussion instruments of present-day orchestras and bands, these drums would seem very strange. They were made of all kinds of materials — tree trunks, logs, pits in the earth, animal skins. Then, too, the early drummers were not concerned with producing sounds that were musically pleasing, for they used their instruments primarily for religious worship and signaling.

Today the picture is quite different. Superior craftsmanship goes into the making of percussion instruments, and a high level of skill and musicianship is required to perform on most of them.

Some percussion instruments have definite pitch and some do not. Of the pitched instruments, the tympani, or kettledrums, are most prominent. The modern instruments are made of large metal bowls with skins stretched over the top. Hand screws are used to vary the tightness of these heads and thus change pitch. You cannot change the pitch of a kettledrum without tuning the drum all over again, and this takes time. So most orchestras have two or more kettledrums tuned to the different notes they will have to play. The drummer has to play a different drum for each note, and it is fascinating to watch him turning from one instrument to another in fast passages. In spite of the limited range that can be obtained on a series of kettledrums, some composers have even used them for short solos. The opening of Beethoven's wonderful violin concerto is a fine example of this use of kettledrums.

The glockenspiel (bells) is an instrument with steel bars arranged like a piano keyboard. It is played by striking the bars with small wooden hammers. The bright tone of this instrument is at times most effective.

The celesta, which is played like a small piano, is actually a glockenspiel with a very small keyboard. This instrument is used to excellent effect in the *Nutcracker Suite* by Tchaikovsky.

The xylophone is similar to the glockenspiel except that its bars are made of wood instead of steel.

Chimes are a set of metal tubes suspended from a frame and struck by wooden mallets. When played they give the effect of church bells. Tchaikovsky makes good use of them in his *1812 Overture*.

There are many percussion instruments which do not produce a definite pitch. Snare drums and bass drums are found in every high-school band. Snare drums get their name from the "snares" (two or more strings) that are stretched across the lower diaphragm. These strings vibrate when the top is struck, and give the lower diaphragm a higher, brighter tone, so that the drum produces a more pleasing sound.

The bass drum gives out a deep booming sound. It is often used in orchestras, but only to accent the rhythm, or to give an undertone of power in a stirring climax of the music.

Cymbals, which consist of two circular brass plates of almost equal size, are in most bands too. If cymbals are of good quality and are well played, they add much to the musical effect of a band or orchestra performance.

The triangle, which derives its name from its shape, is a small steel bar that is struck with a light metal beater. The tambourine, a small single-headed drum, has metal discs loosely attached to the rim so they "jingle" when the instrument is struck or shaken.

All of the percussion instruments are used sparingly, so that one or two musicians can usually handle all of them. Sometimes they sit for quite a while with nothing to do, and then they may have to jump around from one instrument to another as if they had gone wild.

Some other interesting and useful percussion instruments are the tom-tom, gong, woodblock, rattle, and castanets. Oddly enough, the piano is sometimes classified as a percussion instrument because its strings are struck by hammers.

Hymn to the Night

Henry Wadsworth Longfellow   Richard Donovan

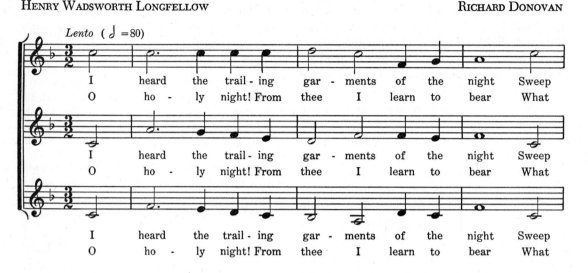

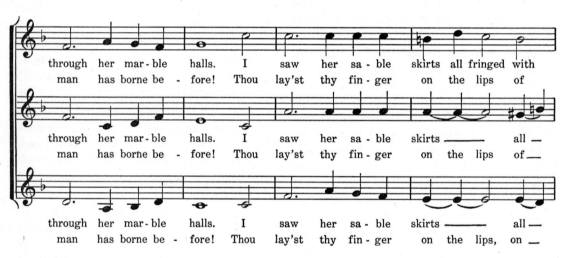

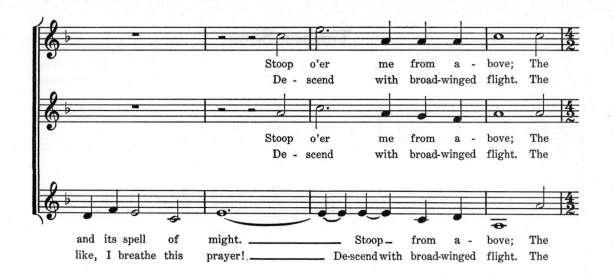

Stoop o'er me from a - bove; The
De - scend with broad-winged flight. The

Stoop o'er me from a - bove; The
De - scend with broad-winged flight. The

and its spell of might. _____ Stoop_ from a - bove; The
like, I breathe this prayer! _____ De-scend with broad-winged flight. The

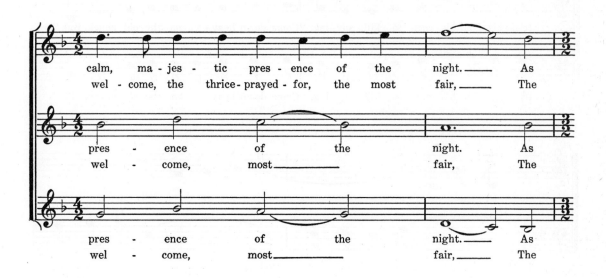

calm, ma - jes - tic pres - ence of the night. _____ As
wel - come, the thrice- prayed - for, the most fair, _____ The

pres - ence of the night. As
wel - come, most _____ fair, _____ The

pres - ence of the night. _____ As
wel - come, most _____ fair, _____ The

rall.

of the one I love, As of the one I love.
best be - lov - ed Night! The best be - lov - ed Night!

of the one I _____ love, _____ As of the one I love.
best be - lov - ed_____ Night!_____ The best be - lov - ed Night!

of the one I love, As of the one I love.
best be - lov - ed Night! The best be - lov - ed Night!

Timber Song

American Folk Song
Arranged by ROY E. FREEBURG

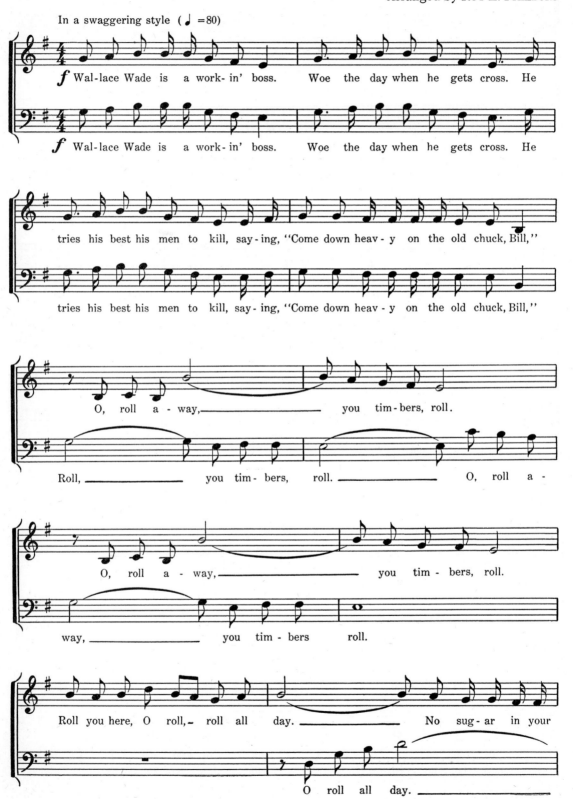

tea,* While work-in' on the Wade Boys' roll-way.

No sug-ar in your tea,* While work-in' on the Wade Boys' roll-way.

O, roll a-way, _____ you tim-bers, roll.

Roll, _____ you tim-bers, roll. _____ O, roll a-

O, roll a-way, _____ you tim-bers, roll, _____

way, _____ you tim-bers, roll, _____ O, roll all

O, roll all day, _____ you tim-bers, roll.

day, _____ you tim-bers, roll.

*pronounced *tay*

After the Revolutionary War, settlers began to move across the mountains in large numbers. Most of them were men of courage and initiative, and a few combined these traits with a spirit of adventure to which the element of danger was an added attraction. In this new country, men and women had to turn their hands and minds to varied and unusual tasks.

The heroes of this period were real people, and the stories of their actual deeds seem almost incredible to us now. The exploits of David Crockett, Daniel Boone, Simon Kenton, Mike Fink, Sam Houston, and others left their marks on the imaginations of even the people who knew them. The legends of these heroes were the beginnings of a new mythology, born of humor and exaggeration.

Chief among the legendary characters was Paul Bunyan, who performed heroic deeds along ordinary lines but magnified a thousand-fold. (See p. 114). Mike Fink (p. 112), however, was a real person, by turns an Army scout, flatboatman, hunter, and trapper.

Lumbering was a job that called for both strength and skill. The pioneers had only their axes to fell the trees, and there are many tall tales of their prowess. The pioneers of America were no less heroic than the characters in the *Iliad* and the *Odyssey*, and they were far more useful to mankind.

Mike Fink

ELOISE LISLE JOHNSON

ELOISE LISLE JOHNSON

Quickly and gaily (♩ =96)

1. Mike Fink, he shot from the boat one day; He aimed at some pigs on the shore, they say! His shot was good and his aim was true; He shot the pig - tails

2. We dance and sing while the fid - dles string, From Pitts - burgh - down to —— New Or - leans! Our keel - boats trim o'er the wa - ters skim, From Pitts - burgh down to

3. In New Or - leans where the life is gay, We danced and —— sang till the dawn of day! But come, my lads, "Good - bye," we say, We'll poke our boats up

Chorus — stanza 3.

3. Pole, boys, we're go-in' up-stream! Pole, boys, we're go-in' home!

Been down to New Or - leans! Pole, boys, pole!

Paul Bunyan

ELOISE LISLE JOHNSON

ELOISE LISLE JOHNSON

spoken

Hi! Babe, my stout blue ox!

Andante (♩ =88)

ff

to — the skies! And then — we'll paint the val - leys green!
fair — and square, My crew's — the fin - est an - y - where!
fig - ure a way, We'll build — our na - tion in a day!

1.

2.

heavily accented   *sf*   *sf*

3.

spoken   *spoken*

Hi! Babe, my stout blue ox!   We've got work to do!

f

Up There

VERNA ARVEY

WILLIAM GRANT STILL

Freely (♩ =84)

Oh, it does no harm to dream that a loft - y fu - ture waits for

WILLIAM GRANT STILL, a leading modern American composer, frequently bases his compositions on Negro themes. Outstanding as an orchestrator and arranger, he has worked in both motion pictures and radio.

Missy Mouse and Mister Frog

American Ballad
Arranged by HERBERT HAUFRECHT

1. O, Miss - y Mouse, I come to see,
2. O, Mis - ter Rat, O he came home,

O, Miss - y Mouse,_ I come to see, if you'd con - sent to mar - ry me,___
Mis - ter Rat,_ O he came home, say'n' "Who's been here since I been gone?"__

too - dee - me - i - dee come to me nay, Fie - id - dle - e day.___

3. There has been here a hand-some man,
4. O, Mis - ter Rat he rode to town,

Fie - id - dle - e - day,___ There O,

There has been here a hand-some man,
O, Mis - ter Rat he rode to town,

Fie - id - dle - e -

has been here_ a hand - some man, I in - tend to get_ him if I can, Sing
Mis - ter Rat_ he rode to town to_ buy his daugh-ter a wed - ding gown,

day___ There has been here_ a man, she'll get him if she can,
O, Mis - ter Rat_ he rode to buy a wed - ding gown,

too - dee - me - i - dee come to me nay, Fie - id - dle - e - day.

p
(melody in alto)
5. O, Mis - ter Frog was dressed in green, Fie - id - dle - e - day,— O,
6. O, just as they sat down for eats, O,
p

poco rit. *mf* *a tempo* *p*
Mis - ter Frog_ was dressed in green And Miss - y Mouse looked like a queen, Sing
just as they_ sat down for eats, Then in came Puss and all her Kits.
mf *p*

too - dee - me - i - dee come to me nay, Fie - id - dle - e - day.

mf
7. O, Puss **took** Rat and Kit took Mouse, Fie - id - dle - e - day,— O,
mf

f
Puss took Rat and Kit took Mouse, And the rest of the com - pa - ny
f

119

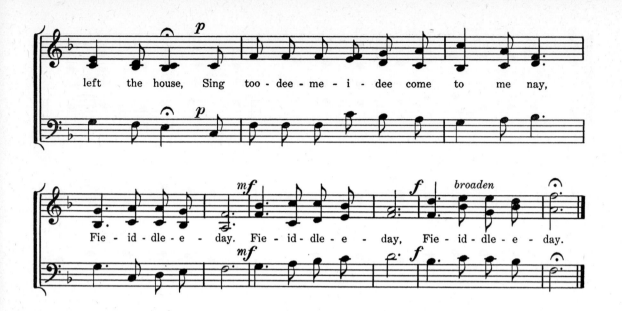

left the house, Sing too - dee - me - i - dee come to me nay,

Fie - id - dle - e - day. Fie - id - dle - e - day, Fie - id - dle - e - day.

Watch America

Most of Morton Gould's music is based on American tunes, and he tries to preserve the American flavor in his style of composition. His *Cowboy Rhapsody*, written in 1942, uses two cowboy songs — *Home on the Range* and *The Old Chisholm Trail*. Mr. Gould was born in New York City in 1913 and was known as a pianist before he became a composer.

ROBERT NATHAN   MORTON GOULD

Where the north - ern o - cean dark - ens, Where the
dark and dream - ing for - ests, By our

roll - ing riv - ers run, Past the cold and emp - ty head - lands Toward the
free and shin - ing seas, By our green and rip - en - ing prai - ries Where the

slow and west-er-ing sun, There our fa-thers long be-fore us, Armed with
west-ern moun - tains rise; God, who gave our fa-thers free-dom, God, who

free-dom faced the deep; What they won with love and la-bor, Let their
made our fa - thers brave, What they built with love and an-guish, Let their

1.
chil-dren watch and keep._____ 2. By our

2.
chil - dren watch and save._____

Dear Land I Adore

W. Otto Miessner   W. Otto Miessner

Alla marcia (♩ =112)

mf

A - mer - i - ca,   dear_ land I a - dore, You are so_ won - drous fair,   How
A - mer - i - ca,   to_   you I'll be true When dan-gers and foes_ as - sail,   My

beau - ti - ful,   How boun - ti - ful!   A   land be-yond   com - pare.   I
loy - al - ty,   My   love for you   Shall nev-er, nev - er   fail.   To

love   your   star - ry flag   So proud - ly   wav-ing there,   The
you,   A -   mer - i - ca,   I vow for - ev - er-more

Papa Tony

Jimmy Eaton, many of whose songs have been on the hit parade, has created in *Papa Tony* a song which is somewhat similar to Italian folk music.

The Recruit

A native Bostonian, Horatio Parker was one of America's outstanding
composers. He was chiefly interested in composing songs and choral works,
and his *Hora Novissima* is one of the finest oratorios of modern times.

A. E. HOUSMAN

HORATIO PARKER

Operetta on the International Stage

It began a long, long time ago — the combination of music and the theatre arts. Some say it started in Greece hundreds of years before the birth of Christ. And still it thrives!

One blend of music and theatre is the operetta, which, as we know it today, is a reasonably short, light work, frequently gay in character. Some authorities claim that *The Beggar's Opera,* written and produced in England over two hundred years ago, was the forerunner of the modern operetta. Others point out that it is not at all similar to operetta but is instead a ballad opera, because its musical numbers are made up of both folk songs and composed tunes. In any event, *The Beggar's Opera* has been conspicuously successful, and to this day is sometimes performed. *Youth's the Season,* which is from the work, is included in this section.

Credit is often given to Franz von Suppé and Jacques Offenbach for being the originators of the operetta. Each man was highly successful in his field, von Suppé writing for the Vienna stage and Offenbach in Paris. *Rondo* from Offenbach's *Bluebeard* is a sample from the operettas written about a hundred years ago.

All are agreed that it was Johann Strauss, Jr., who raised the Viennese operetta to international fame. There is a great appeal and captivating quality about his many popular works. One of his later works, *Die Fledermaus* (The Bat), is still performed many times each year, both here and abroad. The picture on the next page shows a scene from a recent production of it in Central City, Colorado. Sing the *Bell Song* from *Prinz Methusalem* and *Tyrolienne* from *Indigo und die vierzig Rauber* and feel the lilt of each melody, a characteristic of Strauss' music.

While Strauss was writing his operettas in Vienna, a team of Englishmen named Gilbert and Sullivan were turning out the most popular and important English operetta music. Sullivan wrote the music and Gilbert the plays (or librettos). An interesting thing about these men was their dependence upon each other; together they wrote fourteen stage works,

eleven of which were outstandingly successful. Separately, their attempts at operetta-writing were just as unsuccessful as their joint efforts were successful. Their most outstanding works are: *Trial by Jury, The Sorcerer, H. M. S. Pinafore, The Pirates of Penzance, Patience, Iolanthe, Princess Ida, The Mikado, Ruddigore, The Yeomen of the Guard, The Gondoliers.* The wit, sparkle, and satire of these stage works account for the many performances they receive yearly in England and the United States. This section contains two Gilbert and Sullivan songs that you will enjoy: *When I Was a Lad* from *Pinafore* and *Three Little Maids* from *The Mikado.*

Here in the United States at the beginning of the 20th century, two men were famous for their operettas: Victor Herbert, who composed such hits as *The Fortune Teller, Babes in Toyland,* and *Naughty Marietta,* and Reginald de Koven, known best today for his operetta, *Robin Hood.* One of the numbers from this operetta is *The Tinkers' Song,* which you will find in this section.

Later composers of operettas for the American stage are Rudolph Friml, Sigmund Romberg, and Jerome Kern; and still more recent are Richard Rodgers, Leonard Bernstein, Gian-Carlo Menotti, Cole Porter, Kurt Weill, Irving Berlin, and Vincent Youmans.

Even the briefest discussion of the American light opera would not be complete without mention of George Gershwin and his *Porgy and Bess.* Many consider this to be true American opera rather than operetta. The music is filled with the unusual rhythms and melody patterns of American blues and jazz. Both the Broadway stage and Hollywood motion picture studios have produced operettas based on the lives of famous composers. Two notable successes along this line were *Blossom Time,* based on the life and music of Schubert, and *Song of Norway,* about Grieg's life and music. New arrangements of two numbers by Grieg which were used in the *Song of Norway* are included in this section: *Wandering in the Woods* and *Loyal Sons of Glockenheim.*

From a performance of Strauss's *Die Fledermaus* at Central City, Colorado. Photo by Elemer Nagy.

Youth's the Season

From *The Beggar's Opera*
Attributed to JOHN GAY
Arranged by HOWARD LINDBERG

JOHN GAY

Youth's the sea-son made for joys,__ Love is then our__ du - ty.
Let us keep our spir-its__ gay,__ Ours is not to - mor - row.

She a-lone__ who__ that__ em-ploys,__ Well de-serves__ her__ beau - ty.
Love with youth__ flies__ swift a - way,__ Age is nought but__ sor - row.

Let's be gay,____ While we__ may,____ Beau-ty's a flow'r,__des - pised__in de-cay,____
Dance and. sing,____ Time's on the wing,____ Life nev- er knows__the re - turn__of__ spring.__

rit.

Youth's the sea - son made__for__ joys,____ Love is then__our__ du - ty.
Let us keep__our spir - its__ gay,____ Ours is not__to - mor - row.

Bell Song

From the operetta *Prinz Methusalem*

E. Schwab

Johann Strauss

The chap - el bell now

Bong! Bong!

Andantino semplice (♩ =96)

sweet-ly rings with joy - ful chim - ing, The hour clear-ly

Bong! Bong! Bong! Bong! Bong! Bong! Bong! Bong!

tim - ing That to your life new pleas - ure brings; new pleas - ure brings;

Bong! That

a tempo *morendo*

pleas - ure brings.

THE ORCHESTRA — on Stage and in the Pit

Around the turn of the 17th century several things happened of considerable importance for present-day musicians and music lovers. Certainly, one of the most exciting and far-reaching was the beginning of opera. Another, not so dramatic or exciting but no less important, was the first "faint stirring" of the orchestra as we know it today. Our concern is with both of these events because they are so closely related.

It was the work of a man named Monteverdi that got both opera and orchestra off to a good start. In 1607 Monteverdi completed his opera *Orfeo*. This had the same subject and general style as an earlier work called *Euridice*, which had been written by a group of noblemen, artists, and musicians in Italy. However, *Orfeo* was more advanced from the standpoint of both opera and use of orchestra. For the first time, a complete and varied orchestra is used independently, and not as a mere accompaniment. Monteverdi also introduced new effects in his harmony, and this helped him to produce effects of tone coloring that had never been thought of before.

Although large groups of instruments occasionally had been played together, there had been little or no attempt to treat the instruments individually until Monteverdi wrote *Orfeo*.

Even Johann Sebastian Bach and his contemporary, Handel, did little experimenting with new ideas in writing for the orchestra.

By the time Haydn and Mozart reached the musical scene, composers who are little known today had brought about some important changes in orchestral writing, but it was these two masters who did most to establish stringed instruments as the foundation of the orchestra, with woodwind, brass, and percussion used for special effects. Other instruments have since been added, but the basic plan of instrumentation has remained the same.

Today, music played by concert orchestras makes up a sizable part of the world's musical bill-of-fare. Haydn and Mozart would probably be amazed at the size and musical excellence and resources of these great orchestras which are frequently heard in concert, on recordings, and on the radio and television.

Throughout the period of the orchestra's development, composers of theater music have made important contributions to the growth of the orchestra's dramatic and descriptive possibilities. The more influential of these composers were Gluck, Weber, Wagner, and Richard Strauss. At the same time, composers of stage music were quick to utilize the discoveries which had been made by composers of other types of music. Many helpful and mutually beneficial exchanges took place, therefore, between the stage and the orchestra pit.

A rather specialized type of musical composition and arranging for orchestra has existed for some time in the operetta field. A light, gay effect is usually obtained, and you will find this effect especially in the works of Gilbert and Sullivan.

A composer naturally has certain purposes he sets out to accomplish. He wants to heighten the dramatic and musical effect of what is taking place on the stage through the use of the orchestra. At the same time, he cannot take away attention from the stage or cover up the song or speech of the actors. Usually with a small orchestra, he has to try to make his overtures sound as if they were played by a full orchestra, and even here he is still limited by the element of the drama. He cannot excite his audience so much that they experience a great letdown in interest when the curtain is raised.

At no time in history has there been so much theater music as there is today. Background music used so frequently with radio, television plays, and motion pictures serves nearly the same purpose as stage music. It illustrates and adds special emphasis to what is actually taking place in the story.

From time to time some of today's leading composers write musical scores for motion pictures and for radio and television productions. When you watch a motion picture or follow a play or operetta over the radio or television, listen closely to the music to see if it is illustrating and adding emphasis to the story.

The Legend of Madame Angot

From the operetta *La fille de Madame Angot*

English version by Ann MacMillan

Alexandre Le Cocq

1. Just vis-it in the mar-ket Where fish are up for sale, And you will sure-ly see there The la-dy of my tale. And if you can-not spot her by sight, then I sug-

2. She's cross with all the buy-ers No mat-ter who they are; And yet they all a-dore her, They come from near and far. In spring or win-ter sea-son, she'll raise her voice and

3. She'll tell of her ad-ven-tures When she was young and free, In ver-y far off plac-es A-cross the roll-ing sea. She'll tell you of the time when she trav-eled by bal-

gest You lis-ten for a voice__ you can hear from east to west!
yell, And when it seems de- mand-ed, she'll raise her fist as well!
loon, And of her dis-ap- point-ment when it fell down too soon!

rall.

"Fish I sell__ you, fresh! I tell__ you. Buy them now, and don't be slow."
But she's pret-ty and quite wit-ty, And she'll scold you, well we know.
If she's rough,__her friends all suf-fer When her tem-per starts to show.

a tempo
p

She is sau-cy; some what bos-sy, and her name's Ma - dame An-got__
She is rude,__ her chins pro-trude,__her fame is great, Ma - dame An-got__
Still, she's charm - ing, but a-larm-ing, and her name's Ma - dame An-got__

f

Strauss, Die Fledermaus

In the carefree, pleasure-loving Vienna of the second half of the 19th century, the talk at the customary afternoon coffee sessions was largely about the latest operettas and the most recent waltzes.

Perhaps the operetta under discussion was from Paris, or had, at least, been composed by Jacques Offenbach, a German, who had invented the style of "little opera" which made him famous in the French capital. Or it may have been by Franz von Suppé, an Italian-born citizen of Austria. But the most popular composer of operetta was a man who had long been known as a composer of delightful and popular waltzes, Johann Strauss, Jr.

Even the word "waltz" brings to mind the name Strauss, for, as one writer has said, the Strausses of Vienna "set the whole world waltzing."

The elder Johann Strauss helped to turn the 18th century peasant dance, the Ländler, into the most popular dance of his time. But it was Johann Strauss, Jr., his son, who became known as "the Waltz King."

The younger Strauss did not begin to write operettas until he was forty years old, although his publishers and the theater managers had begged him to try his hand at this form of entertainment. The *Tyrolienne* on page 144 is from his first produced work, *Indigo und die vierzig Rauber* (Indigo and the Forty Thieves).

His third, *Die Fledermaus* (The Bat), is the most famous of all his operettas, and is still performed and enjoyed regularly in many countries of the world.

"The Bat" is the nickname of Falke, a character in the play, who had once gone to a fancy-dress ball in the costume of a bat. The complicated story concerns a nobleman who has been sentenced to serve a short prison term on a trifling charge. He goes first with Falke to a fancy-dress ball, and it is there that the mixed-up situations begin.

Here are two melodies from the famous waltz in the overture. This waltz is heard at length in the last part of Act II.

An overture of this kind is like the "preview of coming attractions" in a motion picture theater.

The overture to *Die Fledermaus* begins with a short, fast introduction followed by this melody marked *Allegretto* (not too fast):

The next important theme is:

A slower melody, an *Andante,* is soon heard:

If you ever have an opportunity to see a real performance of *Die Fledermaus* on the stage or over television, be sure to do so. You will find it one of the gayest and most delightful of musical experiences.

Just as we have many kinds of music, so we have many different styles of dancing, several examples of which may be found on neighboring pages.

The Legend of Madame Angot (page 135) is an example of two-part (A-B) form, each period consisting of 16 measures. This is the light musical-comedy type of dancing song. For foot movements use a change step (step, close, step), or a slide. For arm movements, pantomime the words of the song.

Loyal Sons of Glockenheim (page 139) is a marching song. Occasionally the words and notes suggest little running steps (perhaps a bunch of girls fluttering around the soldiers?).

Tinkers' Song (page 147) and *Rondo* (page 152) are operetta selections, with text suggesting the accompanying action.

Three Little Maids from School (page 159): Notice how the piano part describes the simpering, giggling girls.

Youth's the Season (page 131) is English in character and suggests a circle dance with light and dainty foot movements. A floor pattern, based on the phrase pattern (four-measure phrases), might be:

Phrase 1—move clockwise

Phrase 2—return to original position

Phrase 3—move to center

Phrase 4—return to place, with turn in place to close indicating final cadence.

Loyal Sons of Glockenheim

JIMMY EATON

Adapted from Norwegian Dance No. 2
EDVARD GRIEG
Arranged by JOSEPH DeVAUX

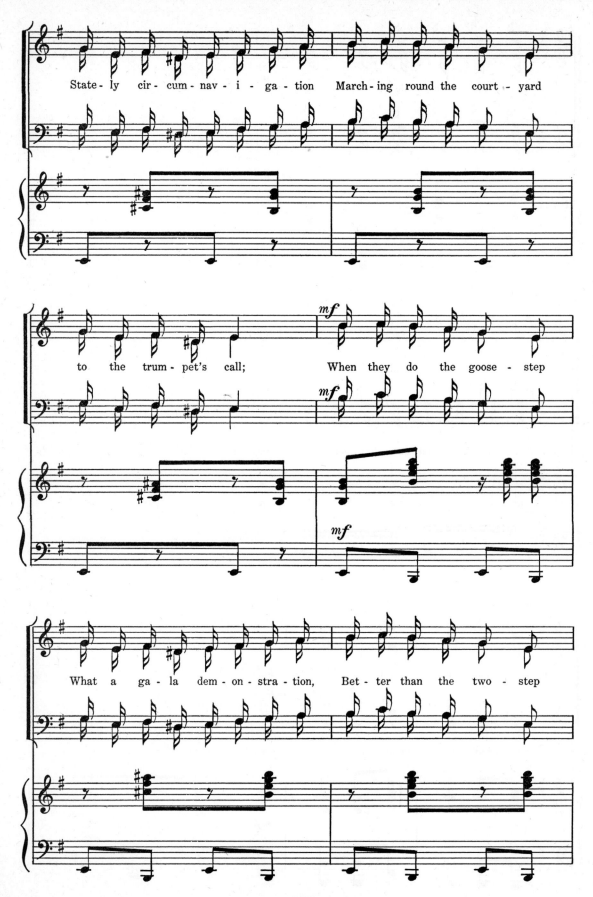

State - ly cir - cum - nav - i - ga - tion Marching round the court - yard

to the trum - pet's call; When they do the goose - step

What a ga - la dem - on - stra - tion, Bet - ter than the two - step

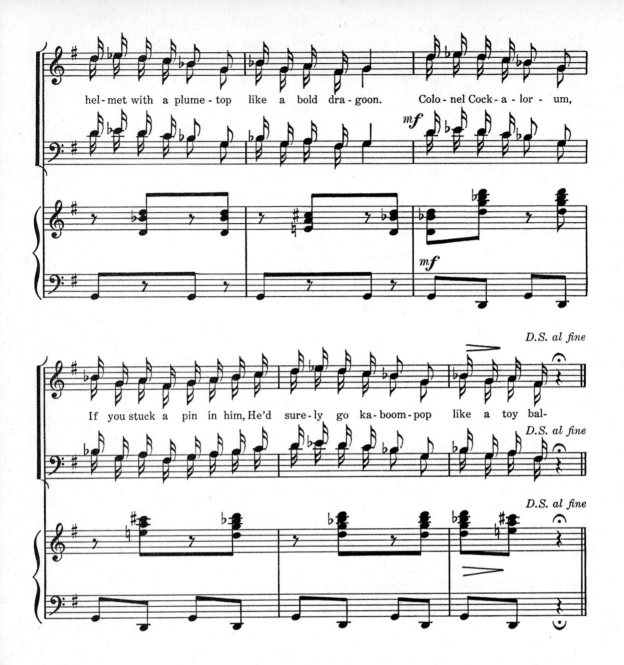

hel-met with a plume-top like a bold dra-goon. Colo-nel Cock-a-lor-um,

If you stuck a pin in him, He'd sure-ly go ka-boom-pop like a toy bal-

D.S. al fine

Tyrolienne

English version by AILEEN FISHER

From the operetta *Indigo und die vierzig Rauber*
JOHANN STRAUSS

Moderato (♩. =50)

Hoop la! And— why are you so sad? Hoop la! A— suit - or should be glad.

Come now, why— must you weep When the whole world is cheer - ful?

Hoop la! You— say you were be-trayed? Hoop la! For - get the faith-less maid,

Find some-one else, find some-one else, Then you'll cease— to be tear - ful.

Tinkers' Song

From the operetta *Robin Hood*

Harry B. Smith

Reginald DeKoven

make us sur - ly— an-swers, We straight-way drown his utt-'rance out by

tap - ping, tap-ping, tap-ping on our pans, sirs! So we rap, rap, rap, And we

tap, tap, tap, From the dawn to the dark of night, sirs, We are

men of met - tle, And the can or ket-tle does-n't live that— we can't right, sirs.

Tink, tank, clink, clank, tink - a - tank - a - tink, tank! Hear our ham - mers

mf sempre staccato e leggiero

ring; When our trade is brisk We frol - ic and we frisk As

f

hap - py and gay as a king.

pp

f

Wandering in the Woods

English version by
NANCY BYRD TURNER

EDVARD GRIEG

tranquillo — — *animato*

sol - i - tude, the love - li - ness, the beau - ty flow - ing free, Are
til a sol - i - tar - y bird be - gins, in trem - bling tone, To
song, the mu - sic as we move, the trees, the love - ly light, Are

like a brid - al ___ gift to bless, a gift for you and me, Are
weave pure mu - sic, ___ word by word, a song for us a - lone; And
made for us a - lone, my Love, are made for us to - night, Are

animato

poco rit. *a tempo*

like a brid - al ___ gift to bless, a gift for you and me.
weaves pure mu - sic, ___ word by word, a song for us a - lone.
all for us, my ___ bride, my Love, are all for us to - night!

poco rit. *a tempo*

p

151

Rondo

Before Jacques Offenbach was of age he was playing in a theatre orchestra. In a short time he was conducting and writing operettas. Thanks to his sparkling tunes, many of his operettas were immediate hits, and were sung all over the world.

The plot of *Bluebeard* does not follow strictly the old tale. In the operetta, Bluebeard is a baron who has already become bored with four of his wives, and has turned them over to the alchemist to be poisoned. Later it is discovered that the wives have not actually been put to death, but have been given a potion which has put them into a long sleep. The wives, awakened from their sleep, come back in the last act for a happy ending.

From the operetta *Bluebeard*

English version by ELEANOR GRAHAM VANCE

JACQUES OFFENBACH

Allegretto grazioso (♩ =152)

She was a love-ly lit-tle Prin-cess, And she was on-ly sweet six-teen. One day two Prin-ces came to see her, And each was look-ing for a Queen. Now

one of these was named Prince Charm-ing; He was hand-some and rich and proud. He

strut-ted through the pal - ace gar - den, And won the fa - vor of the

crowd. The oth - er one was called Prince No - ble, And he was poor and plain, but

kind. He had no thought for his shab - by clothes; He had weight-y

prob-lems on his mind. Prince Charm-ing said, "O love-ly Prin - cess, You know my

name of high de - gree.___ Now where in all the lands a - round us Can you

animato

find an - y one like me?" The Prin-cess turned to face Prince No - ble: "What have

poco meno mosso

you to say? Now don't be shy?" So he said, "I have-n't much to

of-fer, But I will love you till I die." "Your words ring

tru-ly,"said the Prin-cess, "And I will glad-ly be your wife, For wealth and

fame of-ten dis-ap-pear, But our love will last us both for life."

When I Was a Lad

Here Gilbert pokes fun at an office-holder who gets ahead, not by fitness
for the job, but by a reputation gained in other fields.

From the operetta *H. M. S. Pinafore*

W. S. Gilbert

Sir Arthur Sullivan

Allegro non troppo (♩ =104)

Sir Joseph Porter

1. When
2. As

I was a lad I serv'd a — term As — of - fice — boy to an at -
of - fice — boy I made such a mark That they gave me the post — of a

tor - ney's firm. I cleaned the win-dows and I swept the floor, And I
jun - ior clerk, I served the writs___ with a smile so bland, And I

Chorus

pol - ished up the han - dle of the big front door. He
cop - ied all the let - ters in a big round hand. He

Sir Joseph Porter

pol - ish'd up the han - dle of the big front door. I
cop - ied all the let - ters in a big round hand. I

pol-ish'd up the han-dle so ___ care-ful-lee, That now I am the rul-er of the
cop-ied all the let-ters in a hand so free, And now I am the rul-er of the

Chorus

Queen's Na - vee. He pol-ish'd up the han-dle so ___
Queen's Na - vee. He cop-ied all the let-ters in a

care - ful - lee, That now he is the rul-er of the Queen's Na - vee.
hand so free, And now he is the rul-er of the Queen's Na - vee.

Dal Segno 𝄋

Dal Segno 𝄋

Dal Segno 𝄋

3. In serving writs I made such a name
   That an articled clerk I soon became;
   I wore clean collars and a bran new suit
   For the pass examination at the Institute.
      And that pass examination did so well for me,
      That now I am the ruler of the Queen's Navee,
      CHORUS: And that pass examination did so well for he,
            That now he is the ruler of the Queen's Navee.
                                                D.S.

4. Of legal knowledge I acquired such a grip,
   That they took me into partnership,
   And that junior partnership I ween
   Was the only ship that I ever had seen.
      But that kind of ship so suited me,
      That now I am the ruler of the Queen's Navee.
      CHORUS: But that kind of ship so suited he,
            That now he is the ruler of the Queen's Navee.
                                                D.S.

5. I grew so rich, that I was sent
   By a pocket borough into Parliament;
   I always voted at my party's call,
   And I never thought of thinking for myself at all.
      I thought so little they rewarded me,
      By making me the ruler of the Queen's Navee.
      CHORUS: He thought so little they rewarded he,
            By making him the ruler of the Queen's Navee.
                                                D.S.

6. Now landsmen all, whoever you may be,
   If you want to rise to the top of the tree,
   If your soul isn't fettered to an office stool,
   Be careful to be guided by this golden rule,
      Stick close to your desks and never go to sea,
      And you all may be rulers of the Queen's Navee.
      CHORUS: Stick close to your desks and never go to sea,
            And you all may be rulers of the Queen's Navee.
                                                D.C. al Fine

A most important factor in singing a song of this type is the crystal-clear pronunciation of each word, with special attention being given to the words which have sharp final consonants.

Three Little Maids

From the operetta *The Mikado*

SIR ARTHUR SULLIVAN

W. S. GILBERT

Three lit-tle maids from school are we, Pert as a school-girl well can

be, Fill'd to the brim with girl-ish glee,— Three lit-tle maids from school! Ev-'ry-

Unison

thing is a source of_ fun. No-bod-y's

safe, for we care for__ none! Life is a

joke that's_just be - gun!

Three lit - tle maids from school!

Three lit - tle maids who, all un - wa - ry, Come from a la - dies' sem - i - nar - y,

In the operetta, *The Mikado,* the sisters Yum-Yum, Pitti-Sing and Peep-Bo, are wards of Ko-Ko, a tailor who has become mayor of the town of Titipu. The sisters are young and ignorant of the ways of the world, but Yum-Yum has managed to fall in love with Nanki-Poo, who is really the son of the Mikado. But Nanki-Poo has been banished from the court and is earning his living disguised as a trombone player. The accompaniment, as well as the song itself, suggests the three fluttery, giggling girls who view everything as a source of fun.

162

The World Celebrates and Commemorates

What passion cannot music raise and quell?
  When Jubal struck the chorded shell,
  His listening brethren stood around,
And, wondering, on their faces fell
  To worship that celestial sound:
Less than a God they thought there could
    not dwell
  Within the hollow of that shell,
  That spoke so sweetly, and so well.
What passion cannot music raise and quell?

A Song for St. Cecilia's Day
JOHN DRYDEN

Have you ever thought about the indispensable part music plays in the really important occasions of our lives? Can you imagine a wedding without the stirring marches that are generally used at the beginning and the end of the ceremony? Can you picture a patriotic celebration, such as a Fourth of July or Armistice Day parade, without marches or our national anthem? Somehow it would seem as if much of the spirit of the occasion were missing. For most denominations a religious service without music is practically unheard of, and Christmas without its carols just wouldn't be Christmas!

Some of the world's most inspiring music was written for, and is used on, such occasions. The dramatic story of the writing of *La Marseillaise* by Rouget de Lisle and its use during the French Revolution shows the strong effect music can have on people.

Pomp and Circumstance by the famous English composer, Edward Elgar, creates an effect of great dignity and power, and the stirring marches of our own "March King," John Philip Sousa, call forth feelings of patriotic fervor.

One of the most deeply moving of all patriotic compositions is *Finlandia* by the Finnish composer, Sibelius. It was written shortly before the turn of the 20th century when Finland was being ruled by Russia, and the people were in a feverish state of nationalistic, anti-Russian feeling. After *Finlandia's* first performance at a patriotic demonstration, the Russian government banned the work because of its inflammatory effect upon the populace.

From earliest times man has drawn on music to increase the effectiveness of important events. Music has been so closely connected with religious worship that it would be hard to separate either of them completely from the other. The Bible makes frequent references to music and musical instruments, and it is known that over two thousand years ago, music of the Temple in Jerusalem was performed by professional musicians.

As many as 120 silver trumpets called *hasosra chatzotzra* were used at once in King Solomon's day, and powerful pipe organs called *magrepha* and cymbals known as *tziltzal* were also used. One function of these instruments was to announce the entrance of the priests, which was a signal for the congregation to prostrate themselves.

Some authorities believe that the chanting referred to in the Bible was established at least five hundred years before the time of Christ and that a form of it is still sung in some Jewish synagogues today. They also believe that early Christian music owes much to Hebrew music. Christian music was brought together by an official act of Pope Gregory the Great around six hundred years after the birth of Christ. This music, called Gregorian chant, or plainsong, is the basis of Catholic Church music today. The passions and masses of Bach and the oratorios of Handel, Haydn, and Mendelssohn are great musical monuments to man's faith in God and are eternal sources of spiritual refreshment.

Music written to commemorate some of the deepest experiences and most profound occasions in men's lives is offered in the pages of this section. Let us approach this music with a feeling of respect and reverence.

The reproduction of the painting, "Journey of the Magi," by the great 15th century artist, Sassetta, on the next page, suggests a mood that is in keeping with the music in this section.

Detail from "Journey of the Magi" by SASSETTA. From The Metropolitan Museum of Art.

This Is the Day

JAMES BOYD

MARSHALL BARTHOLOMEW

1. This is the day the child was born,　All free from blame,　all
2. There-fore we sing of Thee to - day,　Wher-e'er we are,　wher-
3. And there-on　take good hope a - new From Thy　bright birth,　from

free　from　blame, Who bore the　wound and wore　the thorn　To save the
e'er　we　are, All hum-bly　trust - ing that we　may　Be guid-ed
Thy　bright　birth, That those who　seek Thy will to　do　May to all

free　from　blame,　Who bore the　wound and wore the thorn to save　the
e'er　we　are,　All hum-bly　trust - ing that we may be guid - ed
Thy　bright　birth,　That those who　seek Thy will to do may to　all

sin - ful　and　for - lorn　Who speak　His　name,　who speak　His　name.
by Thee　on　our　way　As　by　a　star,　as　by　a　star.
men and　chil - dren,　too, Bring peace　on　earth,　bring peace　on　earth.

sin - ful　and　for - lorn　Who speak　His　name,　who speak　His　name.
by Thee　on　our　way　As　by　a　star,　as　by　a　star.
men and　chil - dren,　too, Bring peace　on　earth,　bring peace　on　earth.

O Holy Night

Adolphe Adam, son of a musician, lived in the first half of the 19th century. He is remembered chiefly as the composer of light, tuneful operas, the music for *Giselle,* the oldest ballet now performed, and his Christmas song. In his last years he was professor of composition at the Paris Conservatory.

ADOLPHE ADAM   ADOLPHE ADAM

O ho - ly night! — The stars are bright-ly

shin - ing It is the night of the dear Sav-iour's birth;

Long lay the world — in sin and er - ror pin - ing, Till He ap-

166

peared and the soul felt its worth; A thrill of hope the

wea - ry world re-joic - es, For yon - der breaks a new and glo-rious morn.——

Fall———on your knees! O, hear———the an - gel

voic - es, O, night di - vine, O,

night when Christ was born! O, night di -

vine, O, night, O, night di - vine!

Carol of the Birds

Carol from Bas-Quercy
Arranged by PER H. PETERSON

LISTENING NOTES

Sousa, The Washington Post March

John Philip Sousa, America's famous band conductor, was the son of a Portuguese father and a Bavarian mother. He studied music as a small boy in Washington, D. C., and when he was thirteen he enlisted in the Marine Band, an event which shaped his future career. In 1880 he was appointed conductor of the United States Marine Corps Band, and twelve years later he formed his own band, which was to become famous throughout the United States and Europe.

Military music of today dates from the 17th and 18th centuries, when bands became a necessary part of the military equipment in France, Germany, and Great Britain.

The modern "brass band" includes many woodwind instruments, with the clarinets taking the place that violins do in the orchestra. There are also flutes, piccolos, oboes, English horns, trombones, euphoniums, "Sousaphones," and percussion. The Sousaphone, a circular bass tuba built so it can be carried around the body when the player is marching, was made expressly for Sousa's Band in 1899.

Just as Johann Strauss, Jr., was nicknamed "The Waltz King," John Philip Sousa became popular as "The March King." His marches are considered the best of their kind, and at least one of them, *Stars and Stripes Forever,* has become a national patriotic tune. Some others which have won fame are *The High School Cadets, King Cotton, El Capitan, Manhattan Beach,* and *The Washington Post March.*

The *Washington Post March* is named for a newspaper in our nation's capital. This paper had been carrying on a prize literary competition among school children in Washington, D. C., and the day before the winners were to be announced, Sousa was asked to write a march that could be played before the prizes were presented. The *Washington Post March* was written, instrumentated, rehearsed, and performed in less than twenty-four hours. Sousa himself conducted it before an audience of thirty thousand on June 15, 1889.

This new march was greeted with shouts of approval, and it had to be played over and over again. For here was something different! Marches had always been written in 4/4 time. This one, however, was in 6/8 time and was very "marchable."

The first main theme begins like this:

There follows another principal theme, and then, without returning to the opening melody, the march ends with a third theme:

The pattern that gives the music its typical two-step rhythm, which is also a fine rhythm for marching, looks like this:

The typical march rhythm has four beats to the measure, like this:

The two-step rhythm also has two accents to the measure, but the rhythm falls into two groups of three beats each, like this:

In his autobiography, *Marching Along,* John Philip Sousa says, "Like the beat of an African drum, a march arouses the rhythmic feeling in man, and man responds with rhythm."

Good Christian Men, Rejoice!

Ancient German Melody
Harmonized by JOHANN SEBASTIAN BACH

JOHN MASON NEALE

Moderato (♩ =126)

1. Good Chris - tian men re - joice, _____ With heart and soul and
2. Good Chris - tian men re - joice, _____ With heart and soul and
3. Good Chris - tian men re - joice, _____ With heart and soul and

voice; _____ Give ye heed to what _ we _ say: Je - sus
voice; _____ Now ye hear of end - less _ bliss: Je - sus
voice; _____ Now ye need not fear _ the _ grave: Je - sus

Christ is born to - day; Ox and ass be - fore _ him
Christ was born for this! He hath oped the heav'n - ly
Christ was born to save! Calls you one and calls _ you _

bow, And He is in the man - ger now. Christ is
door, And man is bless - ed ev - er - more. Christ was
all To gain his ev - er - last - ing hall. Christ was

born to - day! _____ Christ is born to - day! _____
born for this! _____ Christ was born for this! _____
born to save! _____ Christ was born to save! _____

Carol of the Flowers

English version by
ELEANOR ALLETTA CHAFFEE

Carol from Bas-Quercy
Arranged by PER H. PETERSON

Andantino con espressione (♩ =88)

Lift your fac - es, flow'rs, and praise His shel - t'ring love, That like

rain re - fresh - ing fall - eth from a - bove.

1. Fra - grant vio - let, hid - den in your shad - ed place, Bow your
2. Lil - y cloth'd in sat - in, make the gar - den fair With your
3. Hum - ble pan - sy, smil - ing new each sun - tipp'd day, Let your
4. Rose with vel - vet pet - als, hold with - in your heart All the

poco a poco crescendo

head in wor - ship for His lov - ing grace.
whis - per'd tell - ing of His ten - der care.
bright face show each blos - som how to pray.
gar - den's breath - ing, of His plan a part.

173

Babe of Bethlehem

American Folk Song
Arranged by Joseph DeVaux

Je - sus and— sal - va - tion.   To A - bra -
in the ox - 's man - ger.   No roy - al—
saw and great - ly fear - ed.   The an - gels—
Him God hath— a - noint - ed.   By this you'll .

shin - ing,   shin - ing flame! —   The an - gels

Third verse 8va - - - - - - - - - -

ham the prom - ise— came, and to his seed— for - ev -
things, as used by— kings, were seen by those— that found—
said, "Be not a - fraid, al - though we much— a - larm—
know, if you will— go to see this lit - tle stran -

said, "Be not a - fraid, al - though we much a - larm—

er, A light to shine — in I - saac's line, by
Him, But in the hay— the Stran - ger lay with
you, We do ap - pear— good news to bear, as
ger, His love - ly charms— in Mar - y's arms, both

you, We ap - pear but

scrip - ture we — dis - cov - er.
swad - dling clothes— a - round— Him.
now we will— in - form — you."
ly - ing in — a man - ger."

have no fear."

Jingle Bells

J. Pierpont

J. Pierpont
Arranged by Roy E. Freeburg

O God, Beneath Thy Guiding Hand

JOHN HATTON
Descant by DAVID McK. WILLIAMS

LEONARD BACON

PROCESSIONALS, FESTIVALS, AND PAGEANTS

It is very easy to think of dancing as an expression solely of joy and gaiety, but you may remember that dancing originated in the church, as a natural physical response to deep emotion. Many dances like the Minuet and the Sarabande retain this spirit of dignity, and there is a very real place for rhythmic activity on the most solemn formal or religious occasions. Do not grace and precision heighten the effect of the choir's processional?

On special occasions, and during church festivals, the ordinary processional and recessional may be varied in several ways. For example, those in the procession may walk single file, holding candles. Or they may form a double line, couples linking inside arms, and holding hymn book or music between them with their outside hands. During the processional, foot movements should be exceedingly smooth; whether the upper part of the body moves at all, or sways slightly from side to side, will depend on the wish of the church or congregation. It is possible to be rhythmic and dignified.

When a procession has reached the front of the auditorium, it may continue to a choir loft or stalls, or be dispersed into posed groups, and so on. For the recessional the line is reformed as before.

Perhaps you would like to plan and direct a religious processional. If so, the song *Oh God, Beneath Thy Guiding Hand* (page 180) will make an excellent selection.

In the Middle Ages, in winter, when in northern countries the nights were long and interior lighting was poor, most people went to bed shortly after dark. In the courts of kings and nobles, they would often get up in the middle of the night, have a good meal, and seek entertainment. One activity was the *Torchlight Dance*, a stately procession with music, lit by torches carried by the paraders.

Songs in this part of the book are fine choices for pageant programs.

For a Christmas pageant, see *O Holy Night* (page 166), *This Is the Day* (page 165), *Carol of the Flowers* (page 172), *Good Christian Men, Rejoice* (page 171), *Babe of Bethlehem* (page 174). For a patriotic pageant, see *The Star-Spangled Banner* (page 188), *I Vow to Thee, My Country* (page 186), *National Hymn* (page 190), and *O God of Love* (page 184), especially for Armistice Day. For inclusion in Thanksgiving programs see *Now Thank We All Our God* (page 185); for Easter, *Welcome Happy Morning* (page 196). There are authentic Hebrew melodies on pages 83, 182, and 191.

Many of the English songs and dances in this book may be grouped together for a program. These may be supplemented by a play based on old English customs such as bringing in the boar's head and lighting the Yule Log. You or some one else in the class may have other traditions to suggest.

Do you know about the *Breaking of the Annual Piñata*, a Mexican Christmas custom?

The breaking of the piñata is a regular feature of the Mexican holidays. The Mexican people make many preparations for entertaining, just as we do, the week before Christmas Day. One of the preparations is the hanging of the piñata from the ceiling. The piñata is a container for gifts; it may be a pottery bowl or a brightly colored paper bag.

In the old tradition, groups of people go about singing carols. When the members of a group come to the home of a friend, they knock and are invited to enter. The smallest child is blindfolded and given a stick. Then the child has to find and strike the suspended piñata. When he succeeds, the piñata breaks and the gifts tumble to the floor. Of course there is then a mad scramble! The celebration winds up with gay folk dancing. The dance you learned for the song *The Sierras of Chiapas* (page 36), which is one form of the *Chiapanecas*, is a frequent choice.

A very interesting class project would be to plan a festival program called "Christmas Around the World." For this you could select several typical ceremonies or customs and work each one out as a short scene. Because you would not have time to include all the ideas you might find, select the most colorful for dramatic action, and link the scene by appropriate musical selections for countries not represented by action.

Saleynu (Shabuot Song)

Hebrew words by LEVIN-KIPNIS
English version by HARRY H. FEIN

J. GOROCHOV
Arranged by S. G. BRASLAVSKY

O God of Love

Now Thank We All Our God

CRÜGER—BACH
Arranged by MARSHALL BARTHOLOMEW

CATHERINE WINKWORTH

1. Now thank we all our God, With heart and hands and voices!
   Who wondrous things hath done, In Whom His world rejoices;
2. Oh, may this bounteous God Through all our life be near us!
   With ever joyful hearts And blessed peace to cheer us;

Who from our mother's arms Hath blessed us on our way With
And keep us in His grace, And guide us when perplexed, And

count-less gifts of love; And still is ours to-day.
free us from all ills In this world and the next.

I Vow to Thee, My Country

Cecil Spring-Rice

Gustav Holst

I— vow to thee, my coun-try, all earth-ly things a-
And— there's an-oth-er coun-try, I've heard of long a-

bove, En - tire and whole and per - fect, the serv-ice of my love; The —
go, Most— dear to them that love— her, most great to them that know; We —

Published by J. Curwen & Sons Ltd., London. Used by permission.

love that asks no ques-tion, the— love that stands the test, That—
may not count her ar-mies, we— may not see her King; Her—

lays up-on the al - tar the dear-est and the best; The—
for-tress is a faith-ful heart, her pride is suf-fer - ing; And—

love that nev - er fal - ters, the love that pays the price, The—
soul by soul and si - lent-ly, her shin-ing bounds in - crease, And her

love that makes un-daunt-ed the fi - nal sac - ri - fice. The— -fice.
ways are ways of gen-tle-ness and all her paths are peace. We— peace.

187

The Star-Spangled Banner *(Service Version)*

Francis Scott Key

Attributed to John Stafford Smith

National Hymn

D. C. ROBERTS

HORATIO PARKER

Ba'a M'Nucha (Rest Has Come)

This song, which means "Rest has come," depicts the quiet, inspiring beauty of night-time in the valley of Emek Jezreel. In Biblical times this valley was the granary of ancient Israel. Long neglected, it has now been reclaimed by modern Jewish pioneers who have watered its soil and made it bloom again. In the song, a pioneer professes his love for the Emek, and pledges himself to guard it well.

Hebrew words by N. ALTERMAN
English version by HARRY H. FEIN

D. SAMBURSKY
Arranged by S. G. BRASLAVSKY

1. They who toil are now re - pos - ing;
2. Corn - fields sway in rhyth-mic meas - ure,
1. Ba - a m'nu - cha la - ya - ge - a
2. Yam ha - da - gan mit - no - e - a,

Work is done in field and dell.
Sweet - ly rings the lamb-kin's bell;
U - mar- go - a l' a - mel,
Shir ha - e - der m' tzal - tzel.

Pal - lid night is fast en -
This, the land, this is our
Lai - la chi - ver mis - ta -
Zo - hi ar - tzi us' - do -

clos - ing   Soft - ly E - mek Jez - re - el.
treas - ure,   This is   E - mek Jez - re - el.
re - a   *Al s'dot E - mek Yiz - r' - el.*
te - ha,   *Ze - hu E - mek Yiz - r' - el.*

Moon - lit dew drops glis - ten as they fall,   From Beth Al - fa
Blest be thou, be - lov - ed of us all,   From Beth Al - fa
Tal mil - ma - ta,   ul - va - na me - al   *Mi - Beth Al - fa*
T'vo - rach ar - tzi, v' - tit - ha - lal   *Mi - Beth Al - fa*

Moon - lit drops
Bless - ed be   lov - ed
Tal   *Tal*
T'vo - rach   *ar - tzi*

to Na - ha - lal.   Watch - man,   what of   the night?
to Na - ha - lal.
ad Na - ha - lal.   *Ma,   Ma*   *lai - la   mi - lel,*

THE BAND

No type of musical organization plays as important a part in public celebrations as the band. This has been true for a long time. Henry VIII and Queen Elizabeth of England had bands which played on important occasions, and many rulers since then have followed the same practice. History shows that well over a hundred years ago in Germany a great mass of instruments — one thousand wind instruments and two hundred drums — participated in a celebration to honor a visiting emperor.

The general musical meaning of the term "band" denotes any group of musical instruments. Today, however, we usually use the word in connection with a large group of wind instruments. Here in America we also use the term to denote instrumental organizations specializing in popular dance music — dance bands, jazz bands, swing bands.

Brass, woodwind, and percussion instruments, in various combinations, have been played together for centuries. Before England had her Magna Charta in the 13th Century, princes and others of high degree had their own bands of trumpets and crude kettledrums. Although use of these instruments was restricted to the nobility, a few steps were taken during this same period toward the development of band music. In England, France, and Germany there were pipers who had settled in towns and who did not want to be classed as wandering musicians. These musicians banded together for mutual protection.

Not much distinction was made between the various kinds of musical groups until approximately two hundred and fifty years ago, when three definite types developed — military band, brass band, and orchestra. The concert band, which was an offshoot of the military band, developed later.

The first band of importance in the United States was the U. S. Marine Band founded in 1798. Still in existence, it is one of the country's most respected musical organizations today. An interesting photograph of the band, taken on the Capitol steps, is shown on page 249.

The United States has always been a band-loving nation, and today almost every high school, college, and university can boast of a smartly-uniformed band that is thoroughly trained in marching maneuvers. In addition to playing a big part at sport events and other affairs of their institutions, these colorful organizations frequently fill a real need in their communities by participating in public celebrations of all sorts.

The two men most responsible for band music in the United States were Patrick Gilmore and John Philip Sousa. Both men organized bands which became internationally famous and which influenced the spread of band music to the four corners of the nation. Sousa, an outstanding composer of band music, wrote many marches which are considered among the finest of their kind. Another famous bandmaster, composer, and arranger of music for the band is Edwin Franko Goldman.

Our best concert bands today have a full complement of brass and woodwind instruments: trumpets and cornets, French horns, baritones and euphoniums, trombones and tubas, flutes, piccolos, oboes, clarinets, bassoons, and saxophones, with snare drums, bass drums, cymbals, tympani, triangles, and other types of percussion instruments used for special effects.

While the band movement is now at its peak in American schools, there is a marked decrease in the number of community bands. Fifty years ago practically every village and town had its local band. Many of the players worked at other vocations during the day, but joined in the evening to provide the only music available to the citizens in their communities. There were, of course, no radios and phonographs then. The bandstand was frequently a center for community gatherings of all kinds, and was still to be seen in most towns until quite recently. It symbolized the importance of music in community life. The "town band" made an important contribution to American life, and its decline is a real loss to American music. Perhaps when the many fine players who are now in school bands become adult members of their communities, they will revive this noble American institution.

SINGING NOTES

While we should try to sing all songs as beautifully and with as good tone quality as possible, some songs are better suited for the development of voices than others. There are songs in this section that are particularly effective in this respect.

Welcome Happy Morning by the great English composer, Sir Arthur Sullivan, is not only a wonderful song, but also one that lends itself nicely to vocal study. Notice that the descant in the first two measures is an ascending major scale, the scale of *F* major. Singing scales, if care is taken to make sure that the voice is well supported and the throat is not tight, is excellent exercise. It tends to make the individual tones of a voice more even (alike in quality) and also to increase range. Sing this scale of *F* down several times on "ah" with flowing, free tones. (If the key seems too high, take a lower pitch and gradually work up as high as you can comfortably go.) Then sing the scale up with the same good tone quality. Now sing the first phrase of the descant of the song on "ah"; then sing it with words. Sing the last line of the descant in the same manner. This should result in smooth, even, singing.

Sing the entire descant on "ah," then sing it on other vowel sounds that are comfortable and can be sung with a pure sound, and finally sing it with words. (If the music is too high for some of the voices, they should be allowed to drop out on the high notes. Later, perhaps, these voices can be given the opportunity to sing the descant in a key that is comfortable for them.)

Next sing the melody on "ah" and on other pure vowels and finally with the words. Afterwards, if singers for all parts are available, sing the entire four-part chorus on "ah" with fine broad tones; then repeat it with the words and see that the sustained tones at the end of the phrases are smooth and well supported by breath.

Work on the entire song for fine tone quality and for tone blending. Humming is a good exercise for blending voices. Hum a phrase, then sing the words with the same tone quality and blend of voices that you had while humming.

National Hymn, by the American composer, Horatio Parker, offers an excellent study in sustained singing. It requires a strong, convincing interpretation. Although the climax is at the end of the third line, there is really no unimportant phrase. Sing the song with dignity, using broad, flowing tones; and be especially careful not to force the voice in working towards the climax. Sing each phrase several times on the syllable "ah," or "oh," maintaining an easy, smooth tone throughout the sustained measures.

In the last line, the unison singing should be warm and mellow, though emphatic. A crescendo followed by a soft ending is effective in this phrase.

Try several interpretations and decide upon the one that best expresses the mood and meaning of the text. But always keep in mind the meaning of the words and the feeling of the music in your various interpretations, so that words and music seem to fit together.

Americans should be proud of Horatio Parker, for he was a distinguished American composer and musician, and was honored in England and Europe at great festivals through performances of his compositions. Such honor has rarely been accorded Americans.

Gustav Holst, a modern English composer, has written many beautiful compositions. The second page of his *I Vow to Thee, My Country* is very good singing material for boys whose voices, if not already showing change, will soon start to become lower. The boys should sing the entire second page, using the syllables "ah," "oh," and "nee," in turn. None of the low tones should be forced.

Singing the scale downward from *C*, third space, (then from *B*, B-flat, *A*, A-flat, and finally *G*) will be helpful to them in training the lower compass of the voice and will promote easier and smoother singing in that range. But care must be taken not to force any of the tones.

With all our vocal exercises, we must remember that our purpose is not merely to gain in ability to produce more beautiful tones, but rather it is to improve our voices so that we can sing more musically and with greater pleasure.

Welcome Happy Morning

From the Latin of VENANTIUS HONORIUS FORTUNATUS
English version by JOHN ELLERTON

ARTHUR SEYMOUR SULLIVAN
Descant by J. H. OSSEWAARDE

Allegro giojoso (♩ =92)

Descant (optional)

2. Months in due suc - ces - sion, days of length -'ning light, Hours and pass - ing

1. "Wel - come, hap - py morn - ing!" age to age shall say: Hell to-day is
2. Months in due suc - ces - sion, days of length -'ning light, Hours and pass - ing

mo - ments praise Thee in their flight. Bright-ness of the morn - ing,

van-quished, heav'n is won to - day! Lo! the dead is liv - ing,
mo - ments praise Thee in their flight. Bright-ness of the morn - ing,

sky and fields and sea, Vanquish-er of dark-ness bring their praise to Thee.

God for - ev - er - more! Him their true Cre - a - tor, all His works a - dore!
sky and fields and sea, Vanquish-er of dark-ness, bring their praise to Thee.

Refrain

"Wel - come, hap - py morn - ing!" age to age shall say. A - men.

Refrain

"Wel - come, hap - py morn - ing!" age to age shall say. A - men.

Immortals of Music

Sweet sounds, oh, beautiful music, do not
   cease!
Reject me not into the world again.
With you alone is excellence and peace,
Mankind made plausible, his purpose plain.
Enchanted in your air benign and shrewd,
With limbs a-sprawl and empty faces pale,
The spiteful and the stingy and the rude
Sleep like the scullions in the fairy-tale.
This moment is the best the world can give:
The tranquil blossom on the tortured stem.
Reject me not, sweet sounds! oh, let me live,
Till Doom espy my towers and scatter them,
A city spell-bound under the aging sun.
Music my rampart, and my only one.

Wouldn't you say that the author was under the spell of music at the time he wrote this poem? What kind of music do you suppose it would take to inspire a person to express emotions so beautifully?

The poem is called "On Hearing a Symphony of Beethoven," and was written by the American poetess, Edna St. Vincent Millay. It takes great music to evoke such poetry. It takes immortal music! It is not very surprising that a great work of art in one field can inspire creative artists in other fields. The painting reproduced in the front of this book, an interpretation of Beethoven's *Fifth Symphony* by Bernard Lamotte, is another example of this influence of one field upon another.

It has frequently been said that music is a product of its time and place; because of this, it expresses all kinds of things about a people—tastes, fashions, feelings, strengths, weaknesses. Mozart's music, for example, brings to mind knee-breeches, powdered wigs, courtly manners, and stately ballrooms. On the other hand, American popular music at the turn of the 20th century makes us think of bicycles, high-buttoned shoes, handlebar moustaches, soda-pop, and ball games. Compare a popular song of today with one of thirty-five or forty years ago if you want some idea of the extent of change.

Many of these changing aspects, however, are of a surface nature. We may change our fashions, customs, kinds of jobs, ways of travel-ing, and even our ideas and attitudes about things, but in many ways we are like our forefathers and like our neighbors in other lands. We have the same basic needs, feelings, and problems. These, we might say, are the universal aspects of life, irrespective of time or place.

Immortal music, that is, music which lives, must do more than express the current and changing phases of a time and a place. It must express some aspect of the universal. Beethoven's symphonies do exactly that. And so does Mozart's music. If Mozart had succeeded in writing only "knee-breeches" music, he and his music would have been forgotten long before now.

The story is told of the great problem that faced Beethoven at the time he composed his *Fifth Symphony*. He was becoming deaf, and the doctors of his time could do nothing about it. A composer who could not hear his own music? What could be a worse fate? The *Fifth Symphony* is thought by many to be an expression of Beethoven's struggle with his own destiny and of his ultimate spiritual victory. But the music expresses much more than just the calamity and conquest of one man. In it one senses the struggle and victory of all mankind. Because of this great universal quality, people are continually inspired by this great music.

The Immortals of Music are those composers whose music, like Beethoven's, has lived beyond their own time. The composers represented in this section largely meet this qualification. There may be others who appeal to you in the same way, and you may make your own choices. As you listen to, and perform, music by these and other composers, keep your own personal list of "Immortals."

Mozart, who is portrayed in the painting by Julian Levi on the next page, is one of the really great "Immortals." The painting shows him at the time he wrote his last opera, *The Magic Flute*. This was shortly before his death, which occurred when he was only thirty-five years of age.

A painting by JULIAN LEVI of Mozart composing *The Magic Flute*.
From the Capehart Collection

Where'er You Walk

GEORGE FREDERICK HANDEL

Alleluia

From the cantata *For Unto Us a Child Is Born*

Johann Sebastian Bach

Arranged by Earl Rogers

English version by Earl Rogers

joy,
Freud',

Thus we shall
der wir ver -

not for - get His name e -
ges - sen soll'n zu kei - ner

- ter - nal.
Stun - de.

mf

no rit.

Country Delight

English version by
ELEANOR GRAHAM VANCE

FRANZ JOSEPH HAYDN

1. Oh far from pain and sorrow I greet each joyful
2. I seek a fav'rite nook And listen to the
3. I love the country dances Where ev'ry one ro-
4. In paths of life so pleasant, I live within the

morrow, For I have spent the night In slumber's deep de-
brook That murmurs on its way Through meadows rich with
mances. I share the music's joy With ev'ry girl and
present. In simple country ways I spend my happy

light.
hay.
boy.
days.

The feeling in my heart, The
Beyond the blue of heaven, Be-
I swing my partner lightly, I
The smallest flow'r that blooms, The

feel - ing in — my heart — Is hap - py, free, and gay. — And
yond — the blue — of heav - en, The sky - lark sings for hours, — While
swing — my part - ner light - ly, And lift — her to the sky, — No
small - est flow'r — that blooms — Has some — de - light to give. — I

in — this mood — so joy - ful, I'll stay — the live - long day; — I'll
lamb - kins play — in pas - tures All bright — with sum - mer flow'rs; — All
pea - sant boy — can beat me, And none — would dare — to try; — And
drink — of life — so deep - ly, For once — is all — we live; — For

stay — the live - long day.
bright — with sum - mer flow'rs.
none — would dare — to try.
once — is all — we live.

pp

A Very Kind Young Couple

English version by
FRANCIS X. NULTY

FRANZ JOSEPH HAYDN

whis-pers— soft- ly, "No."
dawn will— see you out.
think I—mean not love.
pit - y— doth de - cree.

"Bab - et, it's late, just—
For— they are sure that—
A— sil - ly goose you—
We'll— stay and kiss till—

mf

mp

one kiss more." She— whis-pers— soft- ly, "No.
with this moon The— dawn will— see you out."
are," she sighs, "To— think I—mean not love."
cock-crow then, As— pit - y— doth de - cree."

mf

When Haydn was a small boy living in a small town not far from Vienna, a visitor from that city heard him sing and admired his sweet, pure voice. He took Franz back to Vienna with him and had him enrolled in the Choir School of St. Stephen's Church, where he received a good musical education. When his voice changed he had to leave the school. After several years of struggle and hardship his compositions attracted the attention of the wealthy Count Esterhazy. Esterhazy engaged Haydn to work as his private conductor and composer with a small but efficient orchestra and a choir of singers.

Haydn lived with the Esterhazys many years, composing music and conducting. He seldom had a chance to go to Vienna and hear music by other composers, so he was forced, as he said, to be original. On one of his rare visits to the city he met Mozart, and the two became firm friends.

After Haydn left the Esterhazy household he lived in Vienna, but he paid two long visits to London, where he was well received and where he composed some of his best symphonies.

In his old age he wrote two oratorios, *The Creation* and *The Seasons*. The singing experience of his youth gave him an insight into writing for the voice, that is apparent in these oratorios and in his church music and songs.

The orchestra at the Esterhazy palace was small, but it gave Haydn a splendid opportunity to experiment with combinations of instruments.

Haydn was born in 1732, the same year as George Washington, but he outlived Washington by ten years.

Haydn was a very busy composer who produced a phenomenal amount of music. This included 104 symphonies, 16 overtures, 27 concertos for various instruments, over 80 string quartets, almost 200 trios for various instrumental combinations, 52 piano sonatas, 12 masses, a number of oratorios, cantatas, and arias, as well as many smaller works, both vocal and instrumental.

Many of his works are just now beginning to enjoy popular favor with music lovers, and Haydn's music is becoming more and more appreciated.

CHAMBER MUSIC

Chamber music is musician's music! Ask almost any member of a concert or symphony orchestra and you will find that after rehearsals and public performances are over, he frequently gets together with one or more fellow musicians to play chamber music. And with composers, too, this type of music has been a favorite. Practically every great composer for the last two hundred years has written some chamber music.

Until the Renaissance (14th-16th centuries), the development of music had taken place primarily under the sponsorship and guidance of the Church. Around 1600, however, the picture changed, and members of the royal families became the chief patrons of music. Because early church music was mainly vocal, little attention was devoted to instrumental music. But change occurred in this respect also early in the 17th century. Instrumental music came more and more into fashion, and princes and other royalty established their own staffs of musicians as a regular part of their courts. The music establishment at the court of Prince Leopold of Anhalt-Cöthen is probably typical of that period. Johann Sebastian Bach was the director, and there were eighteen members: violinists, violists, cellists, oboists, flutists, bassoonists, trumpeters, an organist, a drummer, and a copyist. The prince himself played the clavier, the forerunner of the piano. It was during this time that Bach composed his *Suite No. 3 in D Major.*

In those days the term *chamber music* was used to distinguish music written for performance in the chambers of royal households from music written for the theatre and for church.

The meaning of the term today has changed. Royal sponsorship has long since disappeared, and chamber music is now played at public concerts. But it is still designed to be heard in comparatively small rooms. Unlike band and orchestra music, chamber music uses but one instrument to a part. The great volume of sound produced by bands and orchestras, which requires large concert halls for comfortable listening, is never produced by a chamber-music group. Their music is characterized by clarity, balance, precision, and careful blending of tones, rather than by volume.

Chamber music originated with Haydn and Mozart, and the pattern set by them has been varied only slightly by later composers. Beethoven added his might to the form, and some of his greatest compositions are chamber works. Other master composers who are especially noted for their chamber music are Schubert, Schumann, Brahms, Dvorak, Franck, Tchaikovsky, and Mendelssohn.

Chamber music is usually classified according to the number of players for which a composition is written. There are trios, quartets, quintets, sextets, septets, octets. Some consider instrumental duets as chamber music; others do not. By far the two most frequent types are the *string quartet,* which consists of two violins, a viola, and a cello, and the *piano trio,* consisting of a violin, a cello, and piano. But all kinds of combinations are used. There are pure string groups, pure woodwind groups, and combinations of the two; frequently, too, the French horn and the piano are used in some of these groups.

Chamber music possesses an intimacy that does not exist in any other kind of ensemble music. There is also an independence between the parts that makes the music of each player interesting in itself. Each musician must play with the skill of a soloist, but at the same time, since there is no conductor, there must be the utmost of cooperation between the performers in the group to produce a unified total effect. The musicians must also learn to blend the tones of their different instruments together to produce harmonious sounds.

It takes careful listening to learn to see the beauties in chamber music, and it takes skillful playing to bring out this beauty. Begin listening to some of the well-known chamber works. You might start with a recording of one of the following: *Andante cantabile* from Tchaikovsky's *String Quartet, Opus 11;* the first movement of the Schumann *Piano Quintet in E-flat;* or the first movement of the Mendelssohn *Piano Trio in D minor.*

Aria

Although he was only twelve years old when he composed this operetta, Mozart had seen much of the world, and was a well-equipped musician. While the music in *Bastien and Bastienne* is well written, it is not difficult, and there are only three characters in the story. Many colleges are currently giving performances of this work.

From the opera *Bastien and Bastienne*
WOLFGANG AMADEUS MOZART
Piano accompaniment by HOWARD LINDBERG

English version by AILEEN FISHER

For my loved one I am yearn - ing,

In her face lies ev - 'ry charm; To her all my

loved ___ one gives me pleas - ure, More ___ than wealth an ___ hun - dred fold, More than wealth ___ an hun - dred fold, More than wealth ___ an hun - dred fold.

Bach, Orchestral Suite, No. 3

In the German language the word "Bach" means a brook or a small stream. Someone once said that Johann Sebastian Bach was not a small stream but a mighty ocean! This pun on the name expresses where he stands in music. He was mighty—one of the greatest musical geniuses of all time.

Bach wrote great and noble music in every form that existed in his day, with the exception of opera. Among his works are cantatas, masses, preludes, fugues, toccatas, chorales, sonatas, concertos, inventions, suites, and partitas, as well as a few more types of composition. All of these types or forms had been written by composers before Bach's time, but when one hears any of these titles one immediately thinks of Bach, the master. He invented no new forms, strange as it may seem, but everything he did was the work of a genius.

Bach wrote many suites. Some of them were called partitas; others were called French suites and English suites. He also wrote four orchestral suites, the third of which we will discuss later. Suites written before Bach were called lessons, exercises, *ordres* in French, and *partien* in German.

The suite was a group of dances and introductory pieces, and was one of the earliest instrumental forms developed before Bach's day.

Bach's *Suite No. 3, in D Major,* is for trumpets, oboes, kettledrums, strings, and *continuo.* In his day and long before, a part called the continuo was written into the score, often with "figured bass," which told a harpsichord or clavichord player what chords to play as an accompaniment. This continuo was also played by the violoncellist, as is the case in this *Suite No. 3.* A slow section in which the melody is played by the oboes and the first violin (see *a* below) is followed by a fast section in which the chief melody is woven in and out among the different instruments like colored threads in the design of a piece of cloth (see *b*). There is a short return, but not an exact repetition of the opening *Grave.*

(a)

(b)

Because of an arrangement for violin and piano, known as *Air for the G String,* the second piece of this suite is one of Bach's best known works. Bach wrote it for strings and continuo. It is in two short sections, each of which is repeated.

Here is how it begins:

In the third, fourth, and fifth movements Bach returned to dance forms with a gavotte, a bourrée, and a gigue.

The gavotte is not too fast and usually has the time signature (¢), called *alla breve,* that is, double time written four quarter notes to the measure but counted as two halves. It is 2/2 instead of 4/4. It starts on the second half of the measure as does this one from Bach's *Suite No. 3.*

Following this musical sentence comes a longer second sentence, below, based on the material of the first. Bach turned the theme upside down to have a contrasting way of stating it, returning quickly to statements that are derived from the original theme.

As a contrast to the first section, a gavotte always has a second section which also has two parts. The second section of the gavotte begins this way:

To complete the gavotte, the first section is repeated, (indicated by *da capo* at the end of the second section).

The bourrée, of 17th century French origin, is similar to a gavotte in rhythm (duple) and character, but is a faster dance and starts with a single upbeat.

The gigue (or jig) usually closes a suite. The name is French, but it was a 16th century Irish or English dance. It is gay, fast, and humorous, and is a two-part form, often in 6/8 or 6/4 meter. The following are the first few measures of the gigue from this suite. You will feel two beats to the measure at this rapid tempo.

SINGING NOTES

Heinrich Heine's poem *Du bist wie eine Blume* is a favorite with both adults and children in all parts of the civilized world.

Many composers have set this poem to music, but the two best-loved versions are by Robert Schumann, page 216, and Anton Rubinstein, page 218.

Before learning the songs, compare the two compositions. Notice that both are written in 2/4 meter, but the rhythms within the measures are quite different in the two melodies and in their accompaniments. Rubinstein's measure-rhythm is a simple ♩. ♪ , with ♩ | ♩ at the phrase ends. Schumann uses much more complicated and varied internal rhythms:

The accompaniments, too, are very different, the full and connected chords of Schumann giving quite the opposite effect from the thinner disconnected chords in the Rubinstein version.

Since rhythm is a quality of music that strongly determines the mood, these two settings of the same text have resulted in quite different

songs. Notice that Rubinstein indicates a moderate tempo, while Schumann calls for a very slow movement. After you sing the songs with their accompaniments, you will decide how best to show the beauty and mood of each.

But to do this, to bring out the beauty and mood of the two songs, we must pay special attention to certain important aspects of singing. We must sing at all times with fine tone quality. To achieve this we have to listen carefully to our voices and make the quality as beautiful as possible, and at the same time be sure that we do not have a feeling of tightness in our throats. We must breathe deeply but not strenuously, and our voices should be supported with solid, steady breath. We must pronounce all words clearly and distinctly and yet not allow this to destroy the smooth flow of our tones. We must breathe only at the ends of phrases or other musical units, so as to help bring out the meaning of the words and music. And we must think about the meaning of the words and try to express this in our singing. You will want to sing these beautful songs over and over again.

You Are Like a Lovely Flower *(Du bist wie eine Blume)*

Robert Schumann's happy marriage in 1840 inspired him to write such
a great number of songs (among them, *Du bist wie eine Blume*) that he
called 1840 his "song year."

From the German of HEINRICH HEINE

ROBERT SCHUMANN

You seem so like a flow-er, So
Du bist wie ei - ne Blu - me, So

fair, so sweet and pure. The long-ing now to
hold, und schön und rein, ich schau' dich an, und

see you I scarce-ly can en-dure. If
Weh - muth schleicht mir in s Herz hin - ein. Mir

In the two settings of *Du bist wie eine Blume,* you see songs which are through-composed rather than strophic in form. Each line of the poetry is treated individually in its musical setting, and the resulting songs, called art songs, do not repeat musical ideas for the various stanzas of the poetry as do songs in strophic form.

You Are Like a Lovely Flower *(Du bist wie eine Blume)*

From the German of HEINRICH HEINE

ANTON RUBINSTEIN

You seem so like a
Du bist wie ei - ne

flow - er, So fair, so sweet, and pure. _____ The long - ing
Blu - me, So hold, und schön und rein, _____ ich schau' dich

now to see you I scarce - ly can en - dure _____
an, und Weh - muth schleicht mir in s Herz hin - ein. _____

If I could ask an-y bless - ing, My prayer would
Mir ist, als ob ich die Hän - de auf's Haupt dir

nev - er cease ———— To ask of the Fa - ther in heav -
le - gen sollt',———— be - tend, dass Gott dich er - hal

en To keep you now—— in peace.———— To ask of the
te, so rein, und schön—— und hold,———— be - tend, dass

Fa - ther in heav - en, To keep you now———
Gott dich er - hal - te, so rein, und schön————

Merkenstein

English version by
ANN MACMILLAN

LUDWIG VAN BEETHOVEN

Un poco moderato (♩. =56)

1. Mer - ken - stein! Mer - ken - stein! You are sum-mer's fair de-
2. Mer - ken - stein! Mer - ken - stein! When at noon the day's bright
3. Mer - ken - stein! Mer - ken - stein! When the fair, bright hours de -
4. Mer - ken - stein! Mer - ken - stein! Night has giv - en earth its

p *dolce*

sign When the sky at dawn-ing blush - es, And the day to full-ness
shine Lights the path on which I wan - der; Makes the heav - en which I
cline, And the twi - light fast is near - ing, Then the can - dle seems so
sign. All the stars are now at - tir - ing. For the night, and for re -

rush - es, And the bloom is on the vine; Mer-ken-stein! Mer - ken-stein!__
pon - der Seem more near and more di - vine, Mer-ken-stein! Mer - ken-stein!__
cheer - ing. Now in peace may I re - cline, Mer-ken-stein! Mer - ken-stein!__
tir - ing. May your calm be ev - er mine, Mer-ken-stein! Mer - ken-stein!__

f **p**

The Sailor

English version by AILEEN FISHER

FRANZ SCHUBERT

Allegro con fuoco (♩ =120)

1. In storm and in tem - pest I toss with my
2. The waves drive my ship as it buck - les and
3. The life of a sail - or is what I like

boat; The rain falls in tor - rents and drench - es my
groans; A - head lie the whirl - pools and reefs with their
best! I give up my com - fort for ven - tur - ous

coat; I lash through the waves with their gal - lop - ing
stones; The rocks from the heights crash and tum - ble near
zest. Let tem - pest and tor - rent at - tempt to de -

This accompaniment adds to the stormy scene suggested by the words.

The Huntsman

English version by ANN MACMILLAN

JOHANNES BRAHMS

My
My

love is a hun - ter, His green coat you see ——
love is a hun - ter. His aim's true, but still ——

And — blue are — his eyes, but his — heart is too
He — charms all — the la - dies wher - ev - er he

free, His — heart is too free.
will, Wher - ev - er he will.

My love is a hun - ter, He hunts with the — hound.—

But— I on - ly want him When— he's — al - tar - bound,

When— he's — al - tar - bound.

On Wings of Song

From the German of HEINRICH HEINE

FELIX MENDELSSOHN-BARTHOLDY
Arranged by MARSHALL BARTHOLOMEW

lo - tus flow'rs all are pin - ing To
in the dis - tance the Gan - ges Flows

lo - tus flow'rs all are pin - ing To
in the dis - tance the Gan - ges Flows

pp

p

poco rit. *a tempo*

see their sis - ter dear.
on, thou'lt hear him well.

see their sis - ter dear.
on, thou'lt hear him well.

poco rit. *a tempo*

1.

dal segno

2. There

2. There

1.

dal segno

3. Be - neath a broad palm— we'll rest us;

3. Be - neath a broad palm— we'll rest us;

Free from the world— we'll seem; Re - joiced that fate— has

Free from the world— we'll seem; Re - joiced— that fate— has

blessed us With such a hap - py dream.——

blessed ——— us With such a hap - py— dream.——

The World Makes Merry

Go north, south, east, or west, and where you find merriment and festivity, you will also find music. Go from the jungles of Africa to a New Year's Eve celebration in an up-to-date New York night club, and you will find the same thing. Drop back into almost any period of history, and your findings will remain unchanged. Regardless of time, place, or stage of development, when people put away their daily cares, they turn to music to enliven their celebrations.

Even with the Puritans this was occasionally true. A writer of the time tells of a May Day celebration at Ma-re Mount, Massachusetts, in 1628. He explains that, to the astonishment and dismay of Governor Bradford, the young people set up "... a goodly pine of 80 foote long" and sang "... good May songs, dancing hand in hand around the Maypole and performing exercises ... with Revels and merriment after the old English costome."

For a long, long time, many people throughout the world have celebrated May Day, and it is interesting to consider how important a part music has played on these occasions.

In many villages of Czechoslovakia a maypole is raised before the window of the most popular girl in the village. Frequently, the maypole is an elaborately decorated small tree. The village band plays in the square, and groups of singers go from house to house singing merry folk songs, like the one on page 240. It is a time of dancing, singing, and rejoicing.

In Helsinki, Finland, university students form into groups early on May Day morning and march to the out-of-door summer restaurants. There they spend the day feasting and singing. In Rumania, too, May Day is celebrated in the country. Picnic lunches are eaten in the fields and meadows, and young and old alike dance and sing to celebrate the coming of spring.

German young people make much of Summer Solstice, June 23rd. On this day they march in large groups to the country, where they build great bonfires in honor of the occasion. After a picnic meal is finished, they sing old folk songs and dance about the fire. Some leap through the flames, and engaged couples try to jump together over the fire. The superstition is that if they succeed, they will never part.

In France, the occasion is celebrated as "St. John's Eve." Wherever possible, bonfires are built near a chapel dedicated to St. John, and the members of the parish supply the wood. After a vesper service the priest lights the fire, and all join in singing hymns and chanting prayers. Some of the embers of the fire are later carried home by the townspeople as a charm against evil.

While music in some form plays a prominent role in all festivals where the people themselves have a part, there are many variations. In some festivals music plays the major part.

Every five years on St. John's Day in Estonia, great national singing festivals are held. Musical groups from many other countries come to take part in the mass singing. It is a very colorful affair because the visiting musicians, as well as the local ones, wear native costumes.

The Welsh *Eisteddfod* is one of the more elaborate music festivals. Today the event opens with horn calls, a speech of welcome, and poems that have been written for the occasion. All kinds of competitions follow—solo and choral singing, harp playing, and so on. The festival is believed to stem from the pre-Christian era, and it is known that at the time Wales was annexed to England, the King decreed that the Eisteddfods be considered official public events.

This section, along with others in the book, contains songs that lend themselves well to festive occasions of light nature. In fact, some of the songs have been used for this purpose in their native lands for many generations.

In his interpretation of Manuel de Falla's *The Three-Cornered Hat*, the artist, Julio de Diego, successfully captured the spirit of merriment which the composer created in his musical work of the same name.

An interpretation of de Falla's *The Three-Cornered Hat* by JULIO DE DIEGO. From the Capehart Collection.

Schnitzelbank

This old nonsense singing game was brought to America from Germany about a hundred years ago. A chart with pictures of various objects is hung on the wall, and the leader points to one picture after another while all sing the cumulative verses, somewhat in the manner of *The House That Jack Built*.

German Folk Song
Arranged by Joseph DeVaux

1. Ei du schö - ne, ei du schö - ne, ei du schö - ne Schnit-zel-bank.
2. Ei du schö - ne, ei du schö - ne, ei du schö - ne Schnit-zel-bank.
3. Ei du schö - ne, ei du schö - ne, ei du schö - ne Schnit-zel-bank.
4. Ei du schö - ne, ei du schö - ne, ei du schö - ne Schnit-zel-bank.

Ist das nicht eine Schnit-zel - bank? Ja das ist eine Schnit-zel-bank.
Ist das nicht ein Hin und Her? Ja das ist ein Hin und Her.
Ist das nicht ein Krum und Grad? Ja das ist ein Krum und Grad.
Ist das nicht ein Gold'-ner Ring? Ja das ist ein Gold'-ner Ring.

Ist das nicht ein Kurz und Lang? Ja das ist ein Kurz und Lang.
Ist das nicht eine Licht-putz-scheer? Ja das ist eine Licht-putz-scheer.
Ist das nicht ein Wa-gen-rad? Ja das ist ein Wa-gen-rad.
Ist das nicht ein Schö-nes Ding? Ja das ist ein Schö-nes Ding.

1. Kurz und Lang un-er Schnit-zel-bank.

2. Licht-putz-scheer, Hin und Her,

Kurz und Lang un-er Schnit-zel-bank.

3. Wa-gen-rad, Krum und Grad,

Ice Cream Man *(Ding-Dong, Ting-a-Ling)*

Jimmy Eaton
Piano accompaniment by Fred Mendelsohn

Jimmy Eaton

cream. Ding - dong, ting - a - ling, ice cream, Ding - dong ting - a - ling.

wrong;

Toss your trou - bles for a "loop;" Give your blues the skids.

Toss your trou - bles for a "loop;" Give your blues the skids.

Have your - self a dou - ble scoop With all those hap - py kids, ting - a - ling, ice

Have your - self a dou - ble scoop With all those hap - py kids. How their

The Cavaliers

Czechoslovakia is a country in which many cultures and traditions are blended. Because of this, the music of this country, particularly the dance music, is full of different forms and rhythms. The differing groups who make up the population of Czechoslovakia have all contributed their various characteristic songs to the folklore.

English version by
MARION BERGMAN

Czech Folk Song
Arranged by ANN MACMILLAN

Swing Canon

In this canon the tune follows itself at a space of half a measure so that the tones come together at an agreeable interval. The text itself explains what is going on.

Roy E. Freeburg

Roy E. Freeburg

In a swing style (♩ =108)

Swing a can - on in a syn - co - pa - ted rhy - thm ____ that goes a -

Swing a can - on in a syn - co - pa - ted rhy - thm ____

round and round a - bout; Now in mi - nor

that goes a - round and round a - bout. Now in

The Spinner

English version by
ANN MACMILLAN

German Folk Song
Arranged by EARL ROGERS

Oliver Cromwell

English Folk Song
Arranged by Lucy E. Broadwood

Oli - ver Crom-well lay bur - ied and dead, (Hee! Haw! bur-ied and
Ol - i - ver rose— and gave her a drop, (Hee! Haw! gave her a

dead!) There grew an old ap - ple tree o - ver his head; (Hee! Haw!
drop!) Which made the old wom- an go hip - pi - ty hop; (Hee! Haw!

o - ver his head!) The ap - ples were ripe and were rea - dy to fall;
hip - pi - ty hop!) The sad - dle and bri - dle they lie on the shelf;

(Hee! Haw! rea - dy to fall!) There came an old wom-an to
(Hee! Haw! lie on the shelf!) If you want an - y more you must

gath - er them all, (Hee! Haw! gath - er them all.)
sing it your - self. (Hee! Haw! sing it your - self!)

The Woodchuck Song

Arr. by OSBOURNE WILLIAM McCONATHY

Lively (♩ =100)

If a wood-chuck could chuck wood, How much wood would a

*United States Marine Corps Band on the steps of the United States
Capitol in Washington, D. C. Major William F. Santelman, director, and
Drum Major Elmer Hansen in the foreground.* This famous band, America's
first musical organization, was founded in 1798, one year after George
Washington retired as first President of the United States. First established
as a fife and drum corps of thirty-two men, it became a brass band four
years later. In 1898, one hundred years after its founding and the year its
most famous director, John Philip Sousa, retired, its membership was
increased from thirty-two to sixty bandsmen.

(Official U. S. Marine Corps Photo, by T/Sgt. Rene Bozzie.)

Arturo Toscanini and the NBC Symphony Orchestra in the famous Radio City Studio 8-H of the National Broadcasting Company, New York. Toscanini's phenomenal career began in Rio de Janeiro when, at the age of nineteen, he saved a performance of *Aida* by substituting for a conductor who had been hissed off the stand. In 1908 he came to the United States to conduct the Metropolitan Opera, and in 1928 he became conductor of The Philharmonic-Symphony Society of New York. Since 1937 he has conducted the distinguished NBC Symphony, founded especially for him. (*Photograph courtesy of the National Broadcasting Company.*)

READING MUSIC

Do you remember that before you started to school you could not read? Your parents probably read the funny paper to you and you just looked at the pictures. After you learned to read, you enjoyed reading all sorts of things, and now you would not think of having anybody read for you.

For years you have been singing, in school and out. You probably learn the songs by hearing someone sing them, or by hearing them at the movies or on radio and television. After hearing a song several times, you know how the melody sounds and can sing it yourself. But wouldn't you like to learn to read music so you can learn new songs yourself?

Reading music is much like reading a book. Instead of using letters to form words, music uses notes (♩) and rests (𝄽) to form patterns of melody and rhythm. The notes and rests are placed on five parallel lines (the *staff*) to tell you how the melody of a song sounds. The notes and rests on the staff are like a picture of the melody. If the melody goes up, the notes on the staff move up; if the melody goes down, the notes on the staff move down.

The Descending Scale

Let's look at the note picture of part of a song you know, *Joy to the World.* Sing the beginning of the song. The words are "Joy to the world, the Lord is come."

The song starts up high and moves down smoothly. This is the *note picture* of that part of the song:

Take a close look at this note picture. The note for the word "Joy" is higher on the staff than any other note. As the melody moves down, the notes follow it down. The note for "to" is on the line below the note for "Joy," and the notes use every line and space as the melody moves down. When we reach the word "come," there are no more lines on the staff, and we must add a small line below the staff. This is called a *leger line.*

Doesn't the notation look exactly like the melody sounds? The melody walks right down the staff, touching every step. The notes of this melody form the *descending major scale.* Watch a piano keyboard while someone plays this melody. Do you see the melody walk right down the keyboard? It is played entirely on white keys, and if you examine the keyboard closely, you will find that all of the keys involved, except those that play "Joy to" (*1-7*) and "the Lord" (*4-3*), have black keys between them. The distance between a white key and a neighboring black key is called a half-step, and the distance between two white keys with a black key between them is a whole step. The distance between white keys where there is no black key between is also a half-step.

Now, look at this melody to find half-steps and whole steps. There are whole steps in all places except between *1* and *7*, and *4* and *3*. Actually, this is the pattern of the major scale, and if you start at the top as "Joy to the World" does, it is a *descending major scale.* If you start on the lowest note and go to the top, it is the *ascending major scale.* Regardless of the note on which you start, if this pattern is followed — that is, whole steps between all steps except *3* and *4*, and *7* and *1*, you have a major scale. When a melody moves in this way, it is called a *scale-wise* melody or a *step-wise* melody because it moves along the scale and skips no step on the staff.

In reading music many people use *singing names* or *syllables.* There is a syllable for each step of the scale. Sing the melody again, and this time use the *singing names* or *syllables.*

Do you notice that once you start singing this melody you want to go on? Just for fun, stop on the way down and see how incomplete it sounds. Now sing the whole passage down to *do.* You feel satisfied to stop there, don't you? That is because *do* is the home note, and it is like the home plate on a baseball diamond. In baseball there are a home plate and three other bases. In the musical scale there are two home plates (*high do and low do*) and six other bases (*ti, la, sol, fa, mi, re*).

There are names for the lines and spaces on the staff. The first seven letters of the alphabet are used to name them (*A, B, C, D, E, F, G*). These are called *pitch names.*

The G Clef

At the beginning of each staff there is a sign called a *clef.* There are other clefs, but this particular clef (𝄞) is the G clef. *Clef* means *key* in the same sense as a key to a door. The clef is the key to the names of the lines and spaces on the staff. The G clef locates the pitch *G* on the second line of the staff. The example below shows that the space above *G* is *A,* the next line is *B,* and so on up the staff, with the pitch names in alphabetical order. Down the staff from *G,* the pitch names are in reverse order.

You can see that *do* and *C* are on both the third

space and on the first leger line below the staff. The melody you have been singing and studying is the descending scale in the key of *C*. *C* is the keynote, and *C* is *do*. Sing the scale using syllables and then sing it using pitch names.

The Ascending Scale

Many melodies move in both ascending and descending scale steps. *The First Nowell* moves upward through the scale. This is a note picture of it:

Sing this passage with words, syllables, and pitch names. The first three notes (1) are the last three notes of the descending scale. Next, you sing the ascending scale of *C* (2). After you sing up to high *do,* the direction changes again and the melody moves down the scale to *sol* (3). Sing the ascending scale with syllables and pitch names.

There are eight tones in the major scale, and you can sing it with numbers as well as with syllables or pitch names.

Practice singing the ascending and descending scale with syllables, scale numbers, and pitch names. You may use any one of these in reading music. But always remember to compare the sound of the scale with the sound of the song from which you learned it.

The I Chord or Do Chord

Can you sing *The Star-Spangled Banner* from memory? Sing the melody for these words:

"O say! can you see, by the dawn's early light,
What so proudly we hailed at the twilight's
last gleaming?"

Does the melody move scale-wise? You probably hear some scale-wise passages in the melody, but also many skips. This is the way this portion of *The Star-Spangled Banner* looks when it is written.

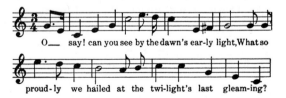

Sing it with syllables, numbers, and pitch names. It begins on *sol (5)*, skips down to *mi (3)* and on down to *do (1)*. It then changes direction and skips up through the same notes to high *do (1)*.

Sing the notes for the words "say can you see." These notes outline a chord which is the *do chord* or *I chord*. It is so named because its first note, or *root*, is *do,* the first degree of the scale.

Sing the melody again to see if you can find other places where it skips through the notes of the *I* chord. Did you observe that it skips through these notes in measures 7 and 8 on the words, "twilight's last gleaming?" (Always start numbering the measures of a song with the first full measure.)

Now sing the *I* chord up and down.

Repeated Tones

You have learned that melodies move scale-wise and by skips. They often have repeated tones also. Can you find repeated tones in this song?

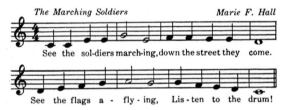

At the beginning, *do (1)* is repeated; there is a skip up to *mi (3)*, and *mi (3)* is repeated; there is a skip up to *sol (5)*, and a skip down to *mi (3)*. What is the chord outlined by these skips?

The remainder of *The Marching Soldiers* moves scale-wise. You should have no trouble singing it if you think of the sound of the ascending and descending scale.

Cadence and Phrase

Look at the words of *The Marching Soldiers.* Do you see that the punctuation divides them into phrases and sentences? When you write language, you use punctuation to make its meaning clear. When you read it, the punctuation helps you to grasp the meaning.

Although there are no punctuation marks in music, the flow of the music in songs usually follows the meaning of the words. In *The Marching Soldiers* the first sentence ends on the word "come." Do you notice that the flow of the music pauses on the same word? This pause in the flow of the music is called a *cadence.* Can you find another cadence in *The Marching Soldiers?* There is another at the end of the song, where you usually find a cadence.

Cadences divide music into *phrases,* and there is a cadence at the end of every phrase. How many phrases are there in *The Marching Soldiers?* There are two phrases, because there are two cadences. The first phrase begins with the first note of the song, and ends at the cadence on the word "come." The second phrase begins on the word "see," and ends at the cadence on the word "drum."

In reading language you grasp the meaning of a whole phrase or sentence. In reading music you should try to hear the sound of an entire phrase.

4/4 Meter

You can march while you sing *The Marching Soldiers* because it has a good marching rhythm. How many steps do you take to each note? Sometimes you take one step for each note, sometimes you take two steps, and on the notes for "come" and "drum" you take four steps.

Sing *The Marching Soldiers* again and swing the rhythm with your hand. When you feel a strong beat, move your hand down; when you feel a weaker beat, move your hand up.

The rhythm of this song swings in four beats: a strong beat, called a *down beat,* followed by three weaker beats. Follow the music as you sing the melody and swing the rhythm. Do you see that there is a line crossing the staff before each down beat? These lines are called *bars.*

The space between two bars is called a *measure.* There are four beats, one strong and three weaker, in each measure of 4/4 meter. The time signature 4/4, placed after the clef, tells you that there are four beats in each measure and that there is a quarter note (♩), or the equivalent, on each beat.

In the first and third measure there is one note on each of the four beats. These are *quarter* notes. When you march to this song, you take one step for each of these notes.

In the second measure there are two *half* notes (♩). You know that one-half equals two quarters, so you can see why there are two steps to each half note, and that each half note is equal to two quarter notes. In the fourth measure there is one *whole* note (o), which lasts through the whole measure (four steps or beats). A whole note is equal to four quarter notes or two half notes.

A whole note is a small oval (o); a half note has a *stem* added to the oval (♩); and a quarter note is like the half note with the oval filled in (♩).

The songs which follow are in 4/4 meter. They move up and down the scale and skip through the *do* or *I* chord. Before you start to sing them, sing the scale and the *do* chord.

253

Key of F

In all the songs we have sung, *do* has been on C, and the songs have been in the key of *C*. There were no sharps (♯) or flats (♭) after the clefs. A sharp placed before a note raises the pitch of that note a half-step, while a flat lowers its pitch a half-step. We can put songs in other keys and move *do* up or down. If there are sharps or flats after the clef, the key is not *C*. Let's see just how this works out.

Do you recognize this song?

It is *The Marching Soldiers*. But it looks different. There is a flat after the clef, and *do* (1) is no longer on *C* but on *F*. To show that a song is in the key of *F* we must place a flat (♭) on the third line (B). This is the *key signature* for the key of *F*.

The scale in the key of *F* looks like this :

The *do* or *I* chord in the key of *F* looks like this when written in separate notes:

Sing the scale of *F* and the *do* chord in the key of *F*. You will hear that they sound higher than in the key of *C*, just as they appear higher on the staff. Otherwise, they sound the same.

3/4 Meter

Sing *Oh, Where Has My Little Dog Gone?* and swing the rhythm with your hand. Is the rhythm the same as in *The Marching Soldiers?*

You feel immediately that *Oh, Where Has My Little Dog Gone* is a waltz rather than a march. Waltz rhythm swings in three beats to the measure, with a strong down beat followed by two weaker beats. The time signature for waltz rhythm is 3/4. This time signature indicates that there are three beats in each measure, and that there is a quarter note, or the equivalent, on each beat.

This is a note picture of the song:

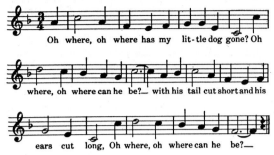

How many cadences do you hear? There are two. The first one is on the word "be." The second one is at the end of the song. Since there are two cadences there are two phrases. Sing each phrase.

The flat after the clef tells you that this song is in the key of *F*. Where is *do (1)* on the staff? What are the notes of the *I* chord? Notice how the melody skips through the notes of the *I* chord.

Sing it again with syllables or numbers, swinging the rhythm as you sing. All our songs thus far, except *The Star-Spangled Banner*, have started on the first beat of the measure. This one starts on the third beat, called a *pick-up*. This means that you will swing two beats before you begin singing on the third beat of the measure.

How many beats do you hold the word "be"? You hold it four beats, three beats in Measure 7 and one beat in Measure 8. In Measure 7 you will see a dot after the half note (♩.). A dot always increases the length of a note by one-half its value. The half note alone would last for two beats; the dot increases its length for a total of three beats.

Notice the arched line between Measure 7 and Measure 8 which connects two notes (♩‿♩). This is a *tie*, meaning that the tone for the word "be" is held for one beat in Measure 8. There is another tie between Measure 15 and Measure 16.

In Measure 16 there is a *quarter rest* (𝄽). A *rest* indicates that there will be no sound for the duration of the rest. For each kind of note there is a rest of the same length. A *whole rest*, like a whole note, lasts four beats, and looks like this: ▬ A *half rest*, like a half note, lasts for two beats, and looks like this: ▬ A quarter rest (𝄽) gets one beat, as does a quarter note.

The V Chord or Sol Chord

The beginning of this song skips up and down through the notes of the *do (I)* chord. Then it steps down to *ti (7)* and up to *do (1)* and *re (2)*. After *re* there are two skips down.

lit - tle dog gone?

This is a new chord. Sing it up and down.

Sol	ti	re	sol	re	ti	sol
5	7	2	5	2	7	5

It is the chord built on *sol*, which is the fifth degree of the scale, and is the *sol* chord or *V* chord in the key of *F*.

Sing the *I* chord and then the *V* chord. After you sing the *V* chord you will probably want to repeat the *I* chord. The *I* chord is the *home* chord, while the *V* chord is an *away-from-home* chord and always tends to go back to the *I* chord. Songs almost always end on one of the notes of the *I* chord.

Now sing the first note, or root, of each chord. Start with *I (do)* move to *V (sol)* and go back to *I (do)*.

Chording

The *I* chord and the *V* chord are the two chords most frequently used in music. By singing the roots of these two chords you can sing another part to many songs. This is called *chording*.

Now let us chord *O Where Has My Little Dog Gone?* Some of the pupils can sing the melody while others sing the chording part, using pitch names, syllables, or numbers.

You will enjoy chording other songs. While doing so, listen closely to the melody, and your ear will tell you which chord fits or harmonizes best with the melody.

Can you write the *I* chord and *V* chord in the key of *C?* They look like this:

Sing the *I* chord and the *V* chord in the key of *C*.

If you can hear and sing the *I* chord, the *V* chord, and the scale, you should be able to read all of the following songs. First look at the key signature to see in what key the song is written. You have read songs in the key of *C* (no sharps or flats), and in the key of *F* (one flat in the key signature). Many of the songs you will want to read will be in keys other than these two, and you will need to be able to tell what key they are in, and where *do (1)* is located.

If there are flats in the key signature, the flat farthest to the right locates *fa (4)*. To locate *do (1)* count down four notes from *fa (4)* to *do (1)*. Do *(1)* is always the key tone.

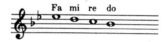

Do is on the third line, *B*. The key is *B* flat.

If there are sharps in the key signature, the sharp farthest to the right locates *ti (7)*. To find *do (1)* you count up one half step from *ti (7)* to *do (1)*. *Do* is the key tone. *High do,* in this example, is on the space above the staff, and *low do* is on the second line. The key is *G*.

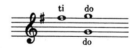

Another way to determine key is to see on what note the melody ends. It will usually end on *do*, the key tone. If it ends on *F*, it is probably in the key of *F;* if it ends on *C*, it is probably in the key of *C*. The next step is to think of the *I* chord and the *V* chord in the key and sing them. Then swing the rhythm for a measure or two and begin singing. You can also chord most of these songs by singing the roots of *I* and *V (do* and *sol)*.

Old Lochaber Lullaby   *Scottish Folk Song*

A Riddle — Czech Folk Song

Our Country — Folk Song from Madrid

My Lambs and My Sheep — Czech Folk Song

Bird Calls — Albrecht

Another Year Is Dawning — Vulpius

Tendencies of Scale Tones

Happy Home of Mine

Jane Rolfe Randolph — Old Song

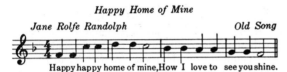

Happy happy home of mine, How I love to see you shine.

Try to sing this new song by following the notation. It begins on *do (1)* and skips up to *sol (5)*. The remainder of the song moves stepwise up to *la (6)* and down the scale to *do (1)* again. Almost every tone is repeated.

Sing it with syllables or numbers. Notice how easily *la (6)* moves down to *sol (5)* on the words "home of mine." *La* is an active tone of the scale and moves down to *sol (5)* which is less active.

Do you hear other tones in the song which sound like active tones? The other active tones are *fa (4)* which moves down to *mi (3)*, and *re (2)* which moves down to *do (1)*. Sing the exercise below and listen for the active tones and the rest tones.

Key of G

Sing *Come, Thou Almighty King* from memory, or have someone sing or play it for you. See if you can tell just by listening whether the rhythm swings in three or four beats to the measure.

This is the notation:

Come, Thou al-might-y King. Help us Thy Name to sing,

Help us to praise. Fa-ther all glo-ri-ous, O'er all vic-

to-ri-ous, Come and reign o-ver us, An-cient of days.

Sing it with syllables or scale numbers. As you can see, the song is in the key of G, and *do* is on G. The key signature for the key of G is one sharp on the fifth line, F.

This is the scale in the key of G:

do re mi fa sol la ti do do ti la sol fa mi re do
1 2 3 4 5   6 7 1 1 7 6 5   4 3 2 1

The notes of the *I* chord and the *V* chord in the key of G are:

I   V

Find the measures of the song in which the melody skips through the I chord. The I chord is outlined in Measure 1 and in Measures 7 and 8 where the melody moves from *sol (5)* down through the notes of the I chord. In Measure 13 the melody skips up through the notes of the I chord. Most of the other notes of this melody move step-wise.

Can you find the active tones and the rest tones? In Measure 2 there is a new active tone, *ti (7)*, which moves up to *do (1)*. We are now acquainted with four active tones in the scale: *re (2)*, *fa (4)*, *la (6)*, and *ti (7)*. The rest tones are the tones of the *I chord: do (1), mi (3)*, and *sol (5)*.

The active tones tend to move to the closest rest tone in the same direction as the melody is moving.

On the first beat of Measure 5 there are two notes called *eighth notes*. Sing the first line of the

song, and notice that these two eighth notes move twice as fast as the quarter notes. At the same rate of speed *(tempo)*, two eighth notes equal one quarter note. To form an eighth note you add a *flag* to the stem of a quarter note (♪). Two eighth notes sung on one syllable are joined by a *beam* (♫). An *eighth rest* looks like this: (↱).

Swing the rhythm as you sing Measures 9 and 10. Do you hear that the notes are not all the same length? The note for the first syllable of "glorious" is held until after the second beat, and the note for the second syllable of "glorious" comes between the second and third beats of the measure.

The notation to indicate this rhythm is a dotted quarter note followed by an eighth note (♩. ♪). Do you recall how a *dot* affects a note? A dot lengthens a note by half its value; in this instance, the dot lengthens the quarter note by half a beat, leaving half a beat for the eighth note. This dotted rhythm is like the rhythm of a skipping step.

The following songs use eighth notes and dotted rhythms. Sing them, using syllables or numbers.

2/4 Meter

Can you sing *The Caisson Song* from memory? If not, perhaps someone will sing it or play the record for you.

Swing the rhythm with your hand. Do you feel that the rhythm swings in two beats to the measure? There is a quarter note, or the equivalent, on each beat. The meter is 2/4.

This is how the first phrase looks. It begins on

the second beat with a pick-up.

When you swing the rhythm, listen carefully to Measure 5 on the words "caissons go." Do you notice that there is no note on the second beat of the measure? There is an accent on the second syllable of cais-*sons* between the first and second beats of the measure, and no accent on the second beat. This is an example of *syncopation,* which means cutting up the rhythm.

The Marines' Hymn is also in 2/4 meter. Sing it and swing the rhythm. Are you aware that it also begins with a pick-up? Is there any difference in the rhythm of the pick-ups of *The Caisson Song* and *The Marines' Hymn?*

From the Halls of Mon-te-zu - ma To the shores of Trip-o-li;—

You have noticed that the first two notes of *The Caisson Song* are of equal length, while in *The Marines' Hymn* the first note is longer than the second. This is another example of dotted rhythm.

Look at the first phrase of *The Marines' Hymn.* To show this fast dotted rhythm, we use a dotted eighth note followed by a *sixteenth note* (♪. ♪).

This is the first time we have studied a sixteenth note. Its stem has two flags. It lasts only half as long as an eighth note. At the same rate of speed (tempo) two sixteenth notes equal one eighth note. A *sixteenth rest* looks like this: (♪).

In Measure 3 there is a dotted quarter note followed by an eighth note. The dotted quarter note is held until after the second beat, and the eighth note comes half way between the second beat and the first beat of the next measure.

In Measure 6 this rhythm is reversed. An eighth note is followed by a dotted quarter note. This results in syncopation, much like that in Measure 5 of *The Caisson Song.* How does it differ?

Sing these two songs and swing the rhythm until you are sure you feel the rhythm of 2/4 meter, and that you understand the notation of the syncopation and the dotted rhythm. Always keep a steady beat.

Here are some songs in 2/4 meter:

If you can remember when you first learned to read language, you will recall that there were some words that you did not recognize. If you came upon these words in your reading, you had to have help before you could pronounce and understand them. You will find this true also in reading music. Many of the songs you are learning will have the same rhythmic and tonal patterns that you have learned, and you will be able to read them all by yourself. Other songs will contain rhythmic and tonal patterns which are unfamiliar to you, and you will need help in learning how they sound. As you have more experience in reading, you will learn many new rhythmic and tonal patterns, and you will be able to sing them when you see them in songs. Reading music is a rather difficult and complex skill. You should not be discouraged if your progress is slow.

There are many songs in this book which you will now be able to read. The following is a list of songs for practice in reading, along with suggestions on each one that will help you to read them.

Lord, Thy Glory, PAGE 2. Key of G 4/4 meter. For beginning pitches sing the *I* chord. The first part begins on *mi (3)*; the second part begins on *do (1)*. The parts move step-wise with occasional skips through the notes of chords *I* and *V*.

Frequent rhythmic patterns:

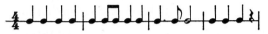

When Love is Kind, PAGE 21. Key of G. 3/4 meter. For beginning pitches sing down from *do (1)* through notes of the *I* chord.

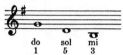

Two upper parts hold *sol (5)*, and lower part holds *mi (3)*. The melody and the counter melody *(descant)* move step-wise and skip through the notes of the *I* chord and the *V* chord. The two lower parts contain chromatics, with which you are unfamiliar. Your teacher will help you with these passages.

Frequent rhythmic patterns:

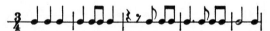

Our Beautiful Valley, PAGE 46. Key of E flat. 3/4 meter.

Scale   I chord   V chord

The beginning pitch is *do (1)*. The melody moves stepwise most of the time.

Unfamiliar tonal patterns:

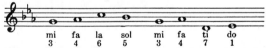

mi fa la sol mi fa ti do
3   4   6   5   3   4   7   1

The melody begins with a pick-up on the third beat of the measure.

Frequent rhythmic patterns:

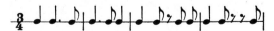

The Linden Tree, PAGE 61. Key of F. 3/4 meter. (Two upper parts.) For beginning pitches, sing up through the notes of the *I* chord. The upper part holds *sol (5)*; the second part holds *mi (3)*. Both parts move step-wise and through the notes of the *I* chord.

Unfamiliar tonal patterns:

mi fa re mi   mi fa re sol
3   4   2   3   3   4   2   5

The song begins with a short pick-up, an eighth note on the second half of the third beat of the measure, before the first beat of the next measure.

A new rhythmic pattern is the triplet (𝅘𝅥𝅮𝅘𝅥𝅮𝅘𝅥𝅮), which has three notes of equal length on one beat. The first of the three notes is accented.

Frequent rhythmic patterns:

Jutlandish Dance Song, PAGE 66. Key of F. 2/4 meter and 3/8 meter. The melody begins on *sol (5)* below *do (1)*. It moves through the *I* chord and along the scale. There is extensive use of the triplet (𝅘𝅥𝅮𝅘𝅥𝅮𝅘𝅥𝅮). The refrain is in 3/8 meter. 3/8 meter swings in three beats to the measure as does 3/4, but in 3/8 meter there is an eighth note, or the equivalent, on each beat instead of a quarter note.

The bass (low) part is written on the bass staff. There are two different notes in the bass part, *do (1)* and *sol (5)*. You can sing it by ear.

Mike Fink, PAGE 112. Key of G. 2/4 meter. There are no unfamiliar tonal patterns, but there is quite a lot of syncopation.

Good Christian Men, Rejoice! PAGE 171. Key of E flat. 3/4 meter. There are no unfamiliar tonal or rhythmic patterns. Above the last note of each phrase there is a *fermata* (𝄐). The fermata indicates that the note under it is to be held for one or two additional beats.

Carol of the Flowers, PAGE 172. Key of G. 2/4 meter. For beginning pitches sing the *I* chord. The soprano part begins on *mi (3)*; second soprano begins on *do (1)*; and the alto begins on *sol (5)* below *do (1)*. There are no unfamiliar rhythmic or tonal patterns.

Oliver Cromwell, PAGE 246. Key of C. 3/8 meter. The melody skips through the notes of the *I* chord. The rhythm swings in three beats to the measure, and there is an eighth note, or the equivalent, on each beat. It usually is faster than 3/4 meter. There are no unfamiliar tonal patterns.

By following this general scheme of finding the key of the song and locating *do*, swinging a few measures of the song to help you feel the rhythm, and going over new tonal and rhythmic patterns before you start to sing, you should be able to read all the songs in the book.

CHORDS FOR ACCOMPANIMENTS

In addition to being able to read songs, you will want to know more about chording. Below you will find notation for several chords in the most commonly used keys. You are already familiar with the *I* and the *V* chords in several keys, and you will find additional chords, valuable for singing as well as for chording with the piano, accordion, guitar, auto-harp and other instruments.

The *IV* chord, built on the fourth degree of

the scale, is used almost as frequently as the *V* chord. Toward the end of a song the V_7 chord is sometimes used. This chord differs from the *V* chord in that it has an additional tone, *fa (4)*. The other chords are valuable to know.

Try using these chords with songs, and let your ear help in deciding which chords to use. Since "barber shop" harmony is based on the use of these chords, you might find it interesting to experiment with harmonizing familiar songs.

ARRANGEMENT INDEX

In this index, the numerals and letters opposite each song title and in the column headed "Classification" are explained in the code below. The numerals correspond to the number of parts in which the song may be sung. For example, "1" — unison, "2" — two-part, and so forth. An asterisk (*) means that an optional descant is available.

The letter which follows a "1" indicates the general range of the melody of the song. Letters following "2", "3", and "4" show the various combinations in which a part may be sung. And the capital letters in the columns 2, 3, and 4 of the code refer to the various types of voices: S Soprano, A Alto, T Tenor, A/T Alto-Tenor, B Bass.

CODE

1. Unison
   a. high
   b. medium
   c. low

2. Two-part
   a. S-A
   b. S-A/T
   c. S-B
   d. T-B
   e. A/T-T

3. Three-part
   a. S-S-A
   b. S-A-A/T
   c. S-A-B
   d. T-T-B
   e. S-A-T
   f. S-T-B
   g. S-A/T-B

4. Four-part
   a. S-A-T-B
   b. S-A-A/T-B
   c. S-S-A-B
   d. S-S-A-A
   e. S-S-A-A/T

GLOSSARY OF UNFAMILIAR TERMS

a' (ä), all (Scotch)
aboon (ă·bōōn'), about (Scotch)

bikurim (bĕ'kŏŏ·rĭm'), a gift offering (Hebrew)
brae (brā), a hillside (Scotch)

Chiapas (chĕ·ä'päs), a state in SE Mexico
Chillon (chĕ·yôn'), a town in Chiapas (Mexico)
Cornish (kôrn'ĭsh), from Cornwall in SW England
coulee (kŏŏ'lē), a trench-like valley

Glockenheim (glŏk'ĕn·hĭm), a mythical kingdom
gold'ner ring (gōlt'nĕr rĭng), a golden ring
grad (grŏd), straight

Helston (hĕl'stŭn'), a town in Cornwall (England)
hin und her (hĭn ŏŏnt hâr), backward and forward
hoolihan (hŏŏ'lĭ·han'), a rowdy person

Jutland (jŭt'lănd), a peninsula in Denmark

krum (krŏŏm), crooked

Leinster (lĕn'stĕr), a province in Ireland
lichtputzscheer (lĭkt'pŏŏts·shĕr'), scissors used at one time to cut the wick of a candle
linden (lĭn'dĕn), a large shade tree
loth (lōth), unwilling, reluctant
Ludlow (lŭd'lō), a town near Shropshire, England

Mancha, La (lä män'chä), old province in Spain
Manzanares (män'thä·nä'räs), a town in Spain
Maxwelton (măks·wĕl'tŭn), a town in Scotland

Merkenstein (mĕr'kĕn·stĭn'), a beautiful spot near Vöslar, Germany
Moo-Lee-Hua (mŏŏ lē whä), a Chinese flower similar to a jasmine
muleteer (mū'lĕ·tēr'), one who drives mules

o' (ŏ), of (Scotch)
Ocosingo (ŏ'kŏ·sĭng'gō), a town in Chiapas (Mexico)
Orestes (ŏ·rĕs'tēz), a legendary character in Greek literature of ancient times

paloma (pä·lō'mä), a dove (Spanish)
philomel (fĭl'ŏ·mĕl), a nightingale
Punchinello (pŭn'chĭ·nĕl'lō), a famous clown

Robin (rŏ'bĭn), a proper name

sae (sā), so (Scotch)
schnitzelbank (shnĭts'ĕl·bänk'), a cutting bench
schönes ding (shāy'nĕs dĭng), a beautiful thing
Shabuot (shä·vŏŏ'ōth), Pentecost, or the Feast of Weeks, in the Hebrew ritual
sierra (sĭ·ĕr'à), a saw (Spanish), usually indicates a range of mountains

wagenrad (vä'gĕn·rŏd'), a wagon wheel (German)

Verdi (vâr'dē), a leading Italian composer of operas
vidalita (vē·dä'lē·tä'), diminutive form of Spanish word for life (la vida)

Zamboanga (säm'bŏ·äng'gä), a province in the Philippine Islands

CLASSIFIED INDEX

National and Ethnical Listings

ALPHABETICAL SONG INDEX

52